196

CORAZON AQUINO

Journey to Power

CORAZON AQUINO

Journey to Power

by Laurie Nadel

Julian Messner ⓂⓂ New York

A Division of Simon & Schuster, Inc.

Library of Congress Cataloging-in-Publication Data

Nadel, Laurie, 1948-
    Corazon Aquino: journey to power.
Bibliography: p. Includes index. Summary: Describes Corazon Aqui-
no's life from her early childhood to her election as president of the
Philippines, including her time spent in the United States and her
marriage to Benigno. 1. Aquino, Corazon Cojuangco—Juvenile litera-
ture. 2. Philippines—Presidents—Biography—Juvenile literature. [1.
Aquino, Corazon Cojuangco.
2. Philippines—Presidents] I. Title.
DS686.616.A65N33 1987 959.9′046′0924 [B] [92] 86-33266
ISBN 0-671-63950-1

Acknowledgments

Many people contributed time and ideas to this book. I would like to thank, especially, Madeleine Morel, Karen Moline, Denise Johnstone-Burt, Phil Van Dijk, Roy Murphy, Helen McNeill, Harlene Brandt, Gayana Gashian, Sal Messina, Susan Shipman, Ginny Puzo, Susan Baumgartner, Jeffrey and Sonia DeChacon, Carmen Ilao Miley, Sister Mary Dolan, Sister Francis Joseph, Terry Stewart, David Hartman, Cindy Coats, Stephanie Abarbanel, Robert Burstein, Jane Pollack, and Gil Quito.

At the Philippine Center in New York, Narciso Reyes and Rose Alcido-Genciana were particularly helpful.

Ike Seneres of the Philippine Embassy in Washington and Leonardo Macariola of the Bureau of National and Foreign Information in Manila also provided assistance.

Corazon Aquino's "fellow Mounties" provided invaluable insight into her college years. The book could not have been written without their help. I am especially thankful to Pat Shea Draddy, Sister Julia Marie Weser, Miriam Vagt, Anita Cipriani, and in Manila, to Sister Virginia Fabella. Sister Virginia went to great lengths to help with this book.

Corazon Aquino's sisters kindly consented to participate in the research. The contribution of their time and recollections is very much appreciated.

My special thanks to James Wentzy whose magic in the darkroom resuscitated some valuable photographs.

For my parents

Contents

CORAZON AQUINO

Journey to Power

O N E

"Co-ry! Co-ry!"

"Co-ry! Co-ry!" The chant filled the grounds and streets around the Filipino Club in the Philippine capital, Manila, on the morning of February 25, 1986. At ten after ten, a white van pulled up, and a diminutive, dark-haired woman dressed in yellow stepped out. She hesitantly waved at the crowd of about three thousand people.

"Co-ry, Co-ry, Co-ry!"

The woman smiled and waved again as hundreds of photographers and cameramen mobbed her. She stepped inside the Filipino Club, a social hall in a prosperous Manila suburb, which was crammed with a thousand more people. As she passed through the doorway, the chant boomed out from the building, "Co-ry! Co-ry!"

News of her arrival flashed around the world, beamed by satellite to television screens in hundreds of different countries.

Inside the Filipino Club, the woman called "Co-ry!" took the oath of office, repeating each

1

Corazon Aquino takes oath of office (with Ninoy's mother in background). February 25, 1986.

phrase after a Philippine judge. When she finished, fifty-three-year-old Corazon Aquino was the president of the Philippines, the first woman to hold that office. She asked people to call her "Mrs. President."

"In the Philippines, two leaders today. Corazon Aquino sworn in as president by a rebel judge," Forrest Sawyer reported on the CBS Morning News program shortly after 7:00 A.M. eastern standard time. "In sharp contrast, Marcos took his oath at the palace."

President of the Philippines since 1965, Ferdinand Marcos and his wife Imelda had governed virtually unopposed for two decades. Theirs was a regime characterized by fierce brutality and corruption. In a report to the U.S. Senate Select Committee on Intelligence, Marcos was described as "a master political tactician who has used his skills to enhance his own power and wealth. But in the process, he has crippled the democratic institutions that were the Philippines' most valued legacy from the American colonial period."

Corazon Aquino, a housewife with no formal political experience, had taken only seventy-five days to topple him after a political confrontation that pitted good and evil against each other.

The day on which both presidents took their separate oaths of office, reports of mayhem and disturbances filtered back to the United States. "The city of Manila can be deceptive," correspondent John Sheahan reported on the CBS Morning News. "You can look out here over the city and it all seems very peaceful. Around the installations held by the Aquino forces, you'll find happy mobs of people. A few blocks away from that, you can find Philippine soldiers of the two factions shooting each other, killing each other." As a result of fighting between Aquino and Marcos supporters, at least ten people were killed the night before the two presidents were sworn in.

A country in turmoil with two heads of state—it was not a situation that could last. Some observers speculated that the United States, which had pressured Marcos into holding elections, would somehow manage to negotiate a settlement between the two leaders. But, as John Sheahan observed, "It's hard to imagine a dignified solution when there's some very undignified killing and dying going on."

Seconds later: "UPI is reporting that President Marcos is willing to leave in exchange for a guarantee of safety for his family."

Where was he going? One big hint came after President Ronald Reagan dispatched his special envoy Philip Habib to Honolulu. Then another bulletin: "Philippine President Marcos is now on his way to Clark Air Force Base, one of the American military bases in the Philippines." Soon after, two helicopters took off from the roof of the presidential palace, and three heavily armed gunboats headed downriver from the palace dock.

"The situation at the presidential palace, as we see it from here now, is pandemonium. We hear frequent, not rapid, gunfire. It is small arms, it is frequent, it is persistent. It is not the kind of gunfire that you would associate with a last stand. It would be a good time for a president to be leaving," Rick Fredericksen of CBS News reported. "The crowds around the palace are sometimes angry. It's not a safe time for journalists there, either."

Philippine soldier takes up position in Manila street. February 1986.

President Ferdinand Marcos and First Lady Imelda Marcos.

Around midnight, Ferdinand Marcos, his wife Imelda, and about ninety family members and supporters left the palace for the last time. They spent the night at Clark Air Force Base, then flew to Guam, finally arriving in Hawaii in a U.S. military C-9 aircraft.

It was a dramatic way for Marcos to concede that he had lost the election. To have remained in the Philippines as anything but the nation's ruler would have been degrading for him.

As the airplane flew him away from the country that he had dominated for so many years, a new era in Philippine politics was starting. Leading it was a soft-spoken woman who had never wanted to be president.

Hundreds of Filipinos stormed the presidential palace soon after the Marcoses left, pushing their way through the gates and climbing onto the balconies. Some went inside, returning with giant por-

Crowds storm Malacanang Palace. February 26, 1986.

traits of Marcos, which the crowd gleefully burned. They waved flags and cheered Corazon Aquino and her vice president, Salvador Laurel.

Corazon Aquino shared their dislike of the palace. During her campaign, she had vowed she would not live in it because it symbolized the wasteful indulgence of the Marcoses, whose extravagance, she said, was bought at the expense of the people's poverty. Instead, Mrs. Aquino had promised to turn the palace into a museum.

One of her first public acts after taking office was to do just that. Thousands of people lined up every day to see the interior of Malacanang Palace, where Ferdinand and Imelda Marcos had lived and entertained.

On view for the first time were the Marcoses' lavish furnishings. There was a private hospital for the ailing president and, in Imelda's suite, treasure beyond imagining. Imelda's closet housed over one thousand pairs of shoes, hundreds of dresses purchased overseas, many still bearing their price tags, and receipts for millions of dollars' worth of jewelry, clothing, and antiques. People cleaning the palace found scrapbooks of photographs of properties in the United States and Europe that belonged to the ousted couple. In the final hours, when rebel troops openly supporting President Aquino were fighting troops loyal to Marcos, neither the president nor the first lady was willing to order the troops to use maximum firepower. "If we wipe them out," Imelda reportedly asked, "what will happen to our assets in the United States?"

Opening the palace confirmed for millions of people that the Marcoses had indeed enriched themselves while the vast majority of the 55 million Filipinos remained impoverished. The Marcos family fortune was estimated at $3 billion, although as president, Marcos's official salary was only $57,000 a year.

T W O

The Early Years

Corazon Aquino's path to the presidency began fifty-three years earlier in Tarlac province, 50 miles north of the Philippine capital, Manila. The woman who was to lead the Philippines was born Corazon Cojuangco, the fourth of six children, on January 25, 1933. Josephine, the oldest, Pedro (Pete), Teresita (Terry), Corazon (Cory), José (Peping), and Pacita (Passy) grew up on a 15-thousand-acre sugarcane plantation. They were by any standards extremely wealthy, especially when their way of life was compared with the severe poverty that most Filipinos endured. Not for Cory and her brothers and sisters the normal chores of taking out the trash and mowing the lawn; servants did those things. Nonetheless, the Cojuangco children were taught to be thrifty.

Corazon's father, José Cojuangco, was a sugar baron who owned not only the plantation where the family lived but also factories and trucks used to transport the sugar. He owned a tremendous amount of land, ran a bank, and served as a congressman from the province of Tarlac. The Cojuangcos were believed to be descended from Chinese traders who had sailed to the Philippines several generations before.

Cory's mother, Demetria (Metring) Sumulong, also came from a wealthy and politically powerful family. Her father served as a senator and, in 1935, ran for vice president of the Philippines. Several of Cory's uncles were also involved in politics, and her father's sister, Isidra Cojuangco, was one of the richest women in the country. Isidra made her mark on Philippine society by founding the Philippine Bank of Commerce with her own money.

Although Cory would later maintain that she had no political experience when she ran for her nation's highest office, she was certainly exposed to politics from a very young age. Her family can be compared to the Rockefellers or the Kennedys of the United States.

Cory's cousin, Sister Virginia Fabella, says that the future president was strongly influenced in different ways by both her parents. "From her father, Cory imbibed a strong spirit of reconciliation. Her father, José, was a quiet, peace-loving man who displayed great patience toward all, who never said a bad thing about another person," she observes.

From her mother, Demetria, Cory and the other children learned to be frugal. "Although the Cojuangcos were a wealthy family, there was never any ostentatious consumption," Sister Virginia notes. Their life-style was simple, even compared with that of other branches of the Cojuangco family. When they went to the movies, they always selected matinees because they were cheaper. And one of Cory's sisters has said that the only luxury she remembers from their childhood was a grand piano.

Cory and her three sisters attended an elite Roman Catholic convent school for girls in Manila, Saint Scholastica's. Each girl received a small daily allowance. Cory wore hand-me-down uniforms that had already been worn by Josephine and Teresita. By the time Cory got them, the seat was usually faded. Even so, her sisters recall Cory complaining about wearing a faded uniform just once.

A quality Cory's mother instilled in her was punctuality and, along with that, self-discipline. Demetria so rarely displayed her feelings that Cory's sisters say they can count on their fingers the number of times they saw their mother cry. Demetria was also strong-willed, a quality that Cory developed and that she learned to hide behind her good manners and soft voice.

Family togetherness was extremely important to the Cojuangcos, as was the Roman Catholic religion. As a young girl, Cory recited the Angelus in Spanish every day, and she and her sisters attended many religious ceremonies. The whole family drove to Sunday mass in a large old car with jump seats so that all seven of them could ride. Her parents followed church teachings and doctrine so closely that Cory and her sisters and brothers were not allowed to go to any movie unless the Catholic magazine, *Commonweal,* had approved it as fit for "general patronage."

At Saint Scholastica's, Cory—who then spelled her name Core and pronounced it CO-ray—was "a quiet, unassuming wisp," according to a fifth grade classmate. Her main extracurricular activity was a game called warball, which resembled volleyball without a net. Apart from her sisters, with whom she was close, Cory did not have any special group of friends. She was a serious student, always reading.

In 1941, when Cory was in fifth grade, the Japanese invaded the Philippines. Cory and the other students had to perform exercises while chanting songs in Japanese. Although neither she nor her immediate family was hurt during the Japanese occupation, her cousins' parents were bayoneted.

Cory's family had moved to Manila and lived there during most of the Japanese occupation, but in 1944 they stayed with relatives in another area. This proved to be a lucky move: their home in Manila was burned down. Its occupants were tied up and killed by the retreating Japanese.

Manila was liberated from the Japanese shortly after Cory's graduation from sixth grade where she was valedictorian. Because Saint Scholastica's School sustained heavy damage in the war, Cory and her sisters transferred to another Roman Catholic girls' school run by the Sisters of the Assumption. Whereas Saint Scholastica's had been run by strict German nuns, the French Sisters of the Assumption believed that education should be enjoyable. They also stressed the importance of social issues, such as concern for the poor.

Cory completed her first year of high school at the Assumption convent. Then, in September 1946, the entire family came to the United States, sailing across the Pacific on an American passenger liner. It was the first time any of the Cojuangco children had traveled abroad. Cory's parents wanted their children to get a better education than they could get in the Philippines, where many of the schools had been destroyed during the war.

In the United States, where Cory's father had many business contacts, the family lived in a residential hotel on New York's West Side. Some of the children attended school in New York, others in Philadelphia.

Since Cory and her sisters had started high school at the Assumption convent in Manila, they enrolled in Ravenhill Academy in Philadelphia, which was run by the same order of nuns. Sister Francis Joseph, who taught the fourteen-year-old Cory in the tenth grade, in 1947, recalls that she and her sisters were placed in a special category with about fifteen students from all over the world who needed to perfect their English. Cory's English improved quickly, and she was able to write good compositions in a short time. She scored in the 80s and 90s in English, Spanish, and geometry. Of all the foreign students, Sister Francis says, the Filipinas were the most keenly aware of the importance of a good education.

Sister Francis remembers young Corazon Cojuangco as "a good thinker, very serious and a very good student." Sometimes perhaps too serious. "I used to encourage her to have fun," Sister

Francis recalls. "She enjoyed cultural outings to plays in New York City and to art museums in Philadelphia, Washington, and New York. She had fine taste." Cory and her sisters also had good taste in clothes. "They were all well dressed and liked fine things," according to Sister Francis.

The students and teachers at Ravenhill formed a close-knit group. Although she was generally quiet, Cory got along very well with many people. And, as at the Assumption school in Manila, she was influenced by the sisters' interest in social issues, especially their concern for the poor. "She was a very loving young woman," Sister Francis remembers.

When she rejoined her family in New York at the end of the school year, Cory took care of her younger brother, Peping, and her sister Passy, cooking breakfast for them and rolling Passy's hair in curlers so it would fall just right, in spirals, the following day. Obedient to her parents' wishes, she nonetheless showed signs of independence and often made her own decisions.

For her sophomore year, Cory enrolled in Notre Dame School in New York City, where her nickname became Cora. When she graduated in 1949, her high school yearbook, *Chez Nous,* had this to say about her: "Beneath her gentle manner lie a friendly disposition and a quiet charm which make her an indispensable part of our group. Pirouetting gracefully in dancing class or deciphering complex 'logs' with fantastic speed, Cora is 'tops' to teachers and fellow students." The book also praised her "energy of true religious faith."

In the autumn of 1949, Cory entered the College

of Mount Saint Vincent, a Catholic women's college at that time, on the banks of the Hudson River in Riverdale, a part of the Bronx, in New York City. The college was founded in 1847 by the Sisters of Charity.

Cory majored in French with a minor in math. Although she excelled at mathematics, she did not want to take the associated science courses. Pat Shea Draddy, a former classmate and now the alumnae director of the college, remembers Cory in math class as "bright and always questioning." Draddy recalls, "She was always there. She was around. She wasn't president of any club or a dynamic leader, but she was lovely and smiling and into everything."

Corazon Cojuangco's high school yearbook picture. Notre Dame Academy, New York City, 1949.

Corazon Cojuangco in the French Club. College of Mount St. Vincents, Riverdale, New York, 1949.

Cory never discussed what, if anything, she planned to do with her French and math after she graduated. Neither subject was considered practical, like nursing, in which forty of Cory's "fellow Mounties" majored. Since she did not have to think about earning a living, she was free to choose whatever courses interested her. In those days, women didn't necessarily plan on a career, so this was not unusual. "When we got out of college we were all considering getting married and raising families," Pat Draddy observes. If nothing else, the story of Corazon Aquino shows that you don't have to know what you're going to be when you grow up in order to achieve greatness later on.

Cory's potential for greatness was not apparent to her fellow classmates. Anita Cipriani, one of the four French majors in Cory's class, recalls that she didn't immediately recognize Cory as her classmate when the news about her campaign for the Philippine presidency started appearing on American TV. Nonetheless, "she was definitely a presence to be felt," Ms. Cipriani remembers, "but she had no need to make noise."

Janet Hannon, who lived in the same dormitory, recalls that Cory "always seemed to have an inner strength, but she gave no hints of being a leader." Miriam Vagt goes further. "She was a quiet little mouse. She was always tailing after her older sister, Terry. It's hard to believe this strong woman came through."

But to Sister Julia Marie Weser, Cory's sophomore English composition teacher, "she was exactly as she is now, except now she is the completely developed woman that she gave every promise of being when she was here. That doesn't mean anyone thought she was going to become the president. She was not easily intimidated, and she was not easily excited. But she had a power and the potentiality."

Outside the classroom, Cory belonged to the French Club; Epsilon Phi, a national honor society; and the Sodality, a Catholic club that emphasized prayer and charitable works. Religious faith was a strong element in Cory's life even when she was a student.

Despite her shyness, Cory and her older sister Terry dressed themselves in traditional Philippine butterfly-sleeve gowns and danced the *tinikling* at a college assembly, hopping over bamboo sticks onstage. Students and teachers present at the time remember that unique performance. "Nobody else ever did that," Sister Julia recalls. "The dance was exquisite."

Corazon Cojuangco in Epsilon Phi, a national honor society. College of Mount St. Vincents, Riverdale, New York, 1952.

Corazon Cojuangco dancing the tinikling with her older sister Teresita (Terry) Cojuangco. College of Mount St. Vincents, Riverdale, New York, 1951.

Apart from that one time, Cory and her sisters did not dress any differently from other students. If anything, they dressed down. "They wore the same clothes all the time. I remember Cory always wore a Mount Saint Vincent's blazer. But they had unlimited charge accounts at Bergdorf Goodman and the other top New York stores," recalls Miriam Vagt.

Cory says that she and her sisters never went overboard when they went shopping. "We were always taught to appreciate what we had and that it had taken my parents so much to be able to give this to us." And, she added, they were expected to be excellent students so that they could rely on themselves—not on the family fortune—later on in life.

So Cory worked hard. But she played hard, too. "The Filipina girls never missed a party," according to Miriam Vagt. "They were the greatest party people you ever met. They enjoyed life in the best way and were extremely well balanced."

Not all of them seemed as smart as Cory, though. Ms. Vagt remembers Cory's cousin Lulu, who wore turtlenecks all the time to cover up the scars left by a Japanese bayonet. Lulu wrote a letter to her boyfriend at Fordham University, which is just a few miles from the College of Mount Saint Vincent. Not knowing Fordham was in the same city, Lulu sent the letter air mail.

Very few Filipinos could afford to go to school in the United States—only the very rich, like the Cojuangcos. However, although it was a poor developing country, the Philippines had a very high standard of education, especially during the post-war years when Cory and her family were studying in the United States.

In many countries around the world, girls were —and still are—not even taught how to read and write. In 1948, when the Cojuangcos were in school, more than half of the women and girls in the Philippines could read and write. That's a very high percentage. There were over 3 million children attending elementary schools in the Philippines, around 200 thousand in high school, and about 6,000 in college. More than 90 percent of those students graduated from all three levels.

To better understand what it was like for an average Filipina girl, let's look at the story of Carmen Ilao Miley. Like Cory, Carmen came from a large Filipino family. She was the youngest of six children. Carmen attended school in Manila in the late 1940s and early 1950s, a few years behind Corazon Cojuangco.

Carmen's father was killed during World War II when she was just four years old. Her mother, who remained a widow, supported the six of them by buying and selling jewelry and odd pieces of real estate. When her mother was granted a U.S. pension because of her father's work in the anti-Japanese resistance movement, the family managed on $200 a month.

Carmen remembers her education as "very good." She attended free public schools where the curriculum for girls emphasized home economics. Boys learned how to do carpentry and other "shop skills." In addition to the "three R's," girls in grammar school were taught how to cook, clean, and sew. "We were taught how to be responsible," she says, adding that the students cleaned their classrooms and their desks. "Both boys and girls took gardening classes and participated in planting contests. The teachers got the asparagus and other vegetables, and the kids got to take home the medals," Carmen remembers.

Although the public schools were not connected with the Roman Catholic church, children did say prayers in school and learned religious songs. Carmen and her brothers and sisters also attended religious instruction and church services.

Carmen, who is now a director of nurses in a New York City hospital operating room, went to high school and nursing school in the Philippines. "No matter how poor you were, there was no such thing as a high school dropout," she says. "Education was really emphasized."

And, as someone who completed her education in the Philippines, Carmen wonders whether the Cojuangco parents sent their children to school in the United States because American schools had more social status. "Some of the schools in the Philippines were burned down and the records destroyed in the war," she concedes. "But many of us managed to get a good education back home, even under those conditions."

After graduating from the College of Mount Saint Vincent in 1953, Cory returned to Manila to study law at Far Eastern University. For a woman to study law was rare in the early 1950s. Only one other member of Cory's college class attended law school.

College yearbook picture. College of Mount St. Vincents, Riverdale, New York, 1953.

But Cory's academic career ended after one year of law school, when she quit studying to marry Benigno Aquino, Jr., a bright, promising young journalist and politician.

Throughout her adult life, Cory often looked back at her school years in the United States with fondness. She may not have used her French or her math very much, but the ethical and spiritual values that were emphasized served her well, providing her with a core of inner strength that would enable her to endure tremendous suffering.

Her education in the United States and her friendships with many Americans would also prove to be important later on. Just as the United States and the Philippines have long been important to each other.

THREE

The Philippines

The Republic of the Philippines occupies a tropical archipelago of 7,100 islands in the Pacific Ocean, about 7,000 miles from Los Angeles and 500 miles off the coast of southeast Asia. Only 2,000 of those islands are inhabited; 2,500 don't even have names, and 500 are less than five square miles in area.

Manila, the capital of the republic, is located on the largest island, Luzon. Although Manila's official population is 1.3 million, the population of Metro (Greater) Manila is 8 million.

The Philippine Islands are home to approximately 55 million people, two-thirds of whom make a meager living from fishing, agriculture (mainly rice), and forestry. The average Filipino earns around $400 a year.

The nation's economy is in deep trouble. The Philippines is the only non-communist country in Asia with a negative growth rate (gross national product, or GNP). That means the nation's ability to sustain itself is declining while its unemployment rate and population are rapidly growing.

A nation of diverse cultures, it is home to a small but powerful wealthy class as well as to primitive tribes who live on remote islands without running water or electricity. Even within Manila, the largest city, there are extreme contrasts between those who live in luxurious mansions and a vast population who inhabits filthy and dangerous slums. In the slum district of Tondo, for example, about 180,000 people crowd into about 17,000 huts jammed into less than one square mile. The majority of the population consists of lower middle-class and middle-class people.

Philippine history goes as far back as paleolithic times—somewhere between 30,000 and 150,000 years ago. Fossils of mammals long extinct and stone artifacts dating from throughout this period have been unearthed from Philippine soil. Human bones 30,000 years old have also been excavated. But some archaeologists say that the first aborigines inhabited the Philippines as recently as 25,000 years ago, after crossing from the Asian mainland on a land bridge. The last land bridge formation linking the islands with the Asian mainland is believed to have sunk into the sea about 5,000 B.C.

Several waves of Indochinese immigrants swept through the country over the centuries. They cultivated rice and built giant terraces for that purpose. Malaysian immigrants brought new trees and new methods of building homes on stilts.

During the Sung dynasty in China (A.D. 960 –1280), Chinese traders sailed to the island of Luzon, trading fine porcelain from China for Philippine wood and gold.

The first Muslims arrived in the fifteenth century, settling in the southern part of the country. They were on the move north when Ferdinand Magellan arrived in 1521. A Portuguese explorer working for the kingdom of Spain, Magellan placed a cross on Philippine soil and claimed the entire territory for the Spaniards. Magellan was killed defending that claim, when a Filipino chief named Lapu-Lapu led his men into battle to contest it.

Twenty-one years later, another Spanish explorer, López de Villalobos, landed in the Philippines and named the islands Las Filipinas after the child who later became King Philip II of Spain. Spain ruled its Pacific colony for more than three hundred years, with the strong companion influence of the Roman Catholic church.

Clark Air Force Base, the Philippines.

Ships docked at Subic Bay Naval Base, the Philippines.

The Filipinos' resentment of Spanish rule intensified during the latter half of the nineteenth century. A nationalist movement dedicated to overthrowing the Spaniards started in 1972 when some arsenal workers staged a mutiny across the bay from Manila. The Spaniards moved in with a vengeance, executing three Filipino priests who had been calling for equality in Philippine society. In 1896, the Philippine Revolution got underway. A strong resistance movement called the Katipunan was discovered by some Spanish friars, precipitating a series of revolts in the provinces around Manila. Several provinces were liberated from Spanish rule and Filipino nationalists declared the first republic in Asia.

Assailed from within the colony, the Spaniards' problems worsened when the Spanish-American

War broke out in 1898. The Spaniards were defeated in Manila Bay by the Americans under the leadership of Admiral George Dewey. Some Filipino nationalists, who did not like the Spanish much to begin with, joined the Americans in fighting them off.

As part of the settlement at the war's conclusion, the United States paid $20 million to Spain for the Philippines, which then became a United States territory. Back home, the U.S. Congress was not particularly enthusiastic about its newly acquired territory. In the Philippines, nationalists who had battled the Spaniards now fought American occupation forces. Fighting continued for several years after the Spanish-American War ended.

During the American territorial period, the United States helped to establish political and governmental models in the Philippines that resembled those in the United States, with the eventual goal of allowing the Philippines to be self-governing. These included reducing the power of the Roman Catholic church so as to make the Philippines a secular state in which government and religion were officially separate; centralizing government administration; improving roads, schools, and other public services; and instituting a two-house legislature made up of a National Assembly and a Senate, much like the U.S. Congress. The Philippine government was also balanced like that of the United States, with an executive, legislative, and judicial branch. As a result of these changes and because of the rapidly growing cities, the Philippine middle class grew much larger and came to include teachers, businesspeople, and government and social workers.

As a step toward full independence, the Commonwealth of the Philippines was established in 1935. This gave the country its own president and vice president, although a U.S. commissioner was appointed to oversee the government there. (It was at this time that Corazon Cojuangco's grandfather ran for vice president.) The President of the United States also retained the right to approve or veto amendments to the Philippine constitution and to approve all financial matters relating to the Philippines. In addition, the United States was also responsible for defending the islands. To that end, American military units remained stationed in the country. To this day, Clark Air Force Base and Subic Bay Naval Base are the largest American naval and air bases outside the United States. One major issue facing the United States is the future of these bases, when the leases come up for renewal in 1991.

Filipinos and Americans fought together to oust the Japanese from the Philippines during World War II. Manila came under attack just ten hours after the Japanese bombed Pearl Harbor, and the Japanese soon occupied the entire country. About one million Filipinos died fighting the Japanese, and by the time the Japanese surrendered on September 3, 1945, Manila was among the cities most thoroughly devastated by World War II.

After the war, the United States kept to its prewar schedule and granted independence to the Philippines. Actually, the first national elections were supposed to take place in 1945, but had to be postponed several months because of war-related disruption. But in 1946, the nation was declared an independent republic and on July 4 of that year, Manuel Roxas was inaugurated as the nation's first president.

In the years following independence, U.S. troops joined Filipinos in battling communist insurgents who were trying to take over the country. The communists are still active in the Philippines. The communist New People's Army numbers about thirty thousand people, and fighting in different parts of the country claims about twelve lives a day. American interests, especially Clark and Subic bases, could be seriously threatened should the communists score any major victories in the Philippines.

FOUR

A Political Marriage

Cory was studying law when Benigno Aquino, Jr., then a reporter for the *Manila Times*, proposed to her. She had met him when she returned to the Philippines after her junior year in college. Ninoy, as he was called, was considered a genius, having graduated from college at seventeen. When he proposed marriage, both he and Cory were twenty-one, although he was born on November 27, 1933 and was therefore eleven months younger.

Cory told him she wasn't ready to be married, even though, as she recalls, "he was the most articulate guy I had met."

Ninoy responded to the initial rejection by teasing her, "If you're such a brain, why couldn't you have gone to better schools in the United States?"

"Maybe they weren't such classy schools," she retorted, "but the underlying values those nuns give you can really help you in life."

Soon she agreed to marry him, and their wedding was one of the most important society events of the

Benigno (Ninoy) Aquino

year. The marriage of Corazon Cojuangco and Benigno Aquino in effect merged three of the Philippines' most influential political families—on Cory's side, the Cojuangcos and the Sumulongs; on Benigno's, the Aquinos.

Benigno's father, Benigno Aquino, Sr., had served as a senator, a speaker of the National Assembly, and a member of the president's cabinet. His grandfather, Sevillano Aquino, was a famous Filipino nationalist who battled first the Spanish and then the Americans. It was his grandfather who nicknamed Benigno Junior "Ninoy," a term of affection that later became a rallying cry for millions of people.

Although Cory wanted a quiet family life, she apparently realized that Ninoy's political ambitions would draw him away from home. That didn't take long. At the age of twenty-two, he ran for mayor of his hometown, Concepción, in Tarlac, the province where he and Cory had grown up.

Their first child, Maria Elena, nicknamed "Ballsy," had just been born when Cory went on the road to help her husband campaign. Filipino politics was a rough-and-tumble business then, as now. Ninoy's opponents had their own private armies of men who drove around in carts, yelling at

President Corazon Aquino and her family. Top, left to right: Benigno Aquino III (Noy), Maria Elena (Ballsy) with Justin Benigno (Signo), Eldon Cruz (Maria Elena's husband), Maria Aurora (Pinky), and Manuel Abelleda (Maria Aurora's husband). Bottom, left to right: Kristina Bernadette (Kris), President Corazon Aquino, and Victoria Elisa (Viel).

people to vote. Ninoy simply made speeches, Cory by his side, shaking hands and smiling. That was all that was expected of her, and it was all she wanted to do. The mere thought of speaking in public terrified her.

"My husband wanted to be number one," Cory admits these days. "But at that time I didn't really mind. He never wanted it said that I was influencing him in anything. I learned soon enough that I wasn't supposed to come out the victor in front of other people. Mine was a private role." Cory believed her main contribution was raising their children—they eventually had four girls and a boy—to be "good and responsible citizens." She kept telling herself, "Someday it will all be worth it."

Ninoy got off to a good start. He won the race for mayor but was later disqualified for having been too young to run at the time of the election. He did get a lot of publicity praising him as a political wonder boy. Cory received word of Ninoy's disqualification with mixed feelings. On the one hand, she shared his disappointment. On the other, she was glad, because it meant that he would have more time for family life.

Although her father had been active in politics, Cory was not prepared to be a political wife. In addition to keeping house in Concepción where there was no electricity from 6:00 P.M., until 6:00 A.M., she had to deal with Ninoy's fellow politicians, aides, and supporters, who roamed through the house, using Cory's kitchen and even walking into her bedroom unannounced. There was no privacy. It irritated her no end at first, especially when people she hardly knew advised her on how to take care of the new baby.

To make matters worse, life in Concepción provided Cory with no intellectual stimulation. She never used her French or math and even forgot how to speak English. Out of sheer boredom, she started listening to soap operas on the radio, soon becoming a soap opera addict. She also went to the movies a lot. Since the chairs in Concepción's only movie house were infested with fleas, she had to bring a raincoat to prevent them from biting her legs.

Losing the mayor's position proved to be a cloud with a silver lining for Ninoy, whose political career quickly took off. At the age of twenty-five, he was executive assistant to the president of the Philippines. At twenty-nine, he was governor of Tarlac province. And at thirty-five, he became the youngest senator in the history of the Philippines. One columnist dubbed him the "Go-go-go senator" because of his seemingly endless energy. Another wrote, "He is married to Corazon Cojuangco, a very charming and a very rich girl—which is not the least of his success."

Ninoy's political beliefs included a strong code of ethics. "When you lose an election, it is as if somebody close to you died, as if part of you died. So you must go out of your way if you are the victor to make amends," he told Cory. Ninoy made sure that he visited each opponent who lost an election to him, to extend his understanding and support. This spirit of reconciliation would continue to be a large part of Ninoy's appeal to the public and would later become his legacy to his people.

By the time Ninoy became a senator, Cory's role had crystallized. "I was simply a politician's wife. I took care of the home and the children, and Ninoy took care of the rest."

One of Ninoy's fellow politicians recalls, "Ninoy and I would talk strategy while she cooked. She would interrupt only to ask us what we wanted to eat. She was a good wife, but she made a poor impression."

Cory was, in fact, so subservient that she would never say anything if Ninoy was around. "I was supposed to just listen, and then in the privacy of our room Ninoy and I would discuss certain things."

But those bedroom briefings stopped in 1972 after President Ferdinand Marcos declared what he called "smiling martial law." Marcos was one of the few people smiling.

The sixth president of the Philippines, Marcos credited himself with having invented a new form of dictatorship, which he called "constitutional authoritarianism." He rewrote the Philippine constitution to give himself virtually unlimited power.

Elected to his first term in 1965, Marcos found himself threatened by an opposition that ran the political gamut from peaceful liberals to armed communist insurgents. More than seventy thousand people were detained without charge, according to a Philippine human rights group, and many of the detainees were beaten and abused during the eleven years of "smiling martial law."

There were no external signs of trouble during this period—no tanks or troops in the streets. But President Marcos closed down the media, dismantled the congress, and jailed political opponents, all of which led one critic to observe that "Marcos's main contribution to democracy was to show how much of it his people had lost."

One of Marcos's more vocal opponents, Senator Benigno Aquino, often spoke out against these abuses of power. For this, he was thrown in jail in 1972, on trumped-up charges of murder, subversion, and illegal possession of firearms. The young senator was being talked about as a possible successor to Marcos if presidential elections were ever held, and as the dictator's main rival, Ninoy had to be silenced.

Ninoy's imprisonment for seven years and seven months changed Cory's life forever. "It was then that I finally came into my own," she says. "I made all the major decisions."

She also learned how few people were her real friends. People who had called themselves friends when Ninoy was a senator literally turned their backs on Cory while he was in prison. Some even crossed the street to avoid saying hello. At first, she would ask herself, "Why does it have to be us?" But her religious background helped her to see the suffering in a new light, and she became more accepting, believing there were lessons to be learned in those times of trouble.

They were difficult lessons. Cory tried to find comfort in prayer, attending mass every day, but she found it hard to concentrate. She and her children often said the rosary in the hope of helping Ninoy. At one point, Cory even told her children that they needed to make sacrifices in order to help bring about their father's freedom. She told them to give up going to parties as she herself had given up going to the beauty parlor and buying new clothes. But a priest suggested that it would be better if she allowed everyone, including herself, to live normally.

After Ninoy had been in prison for a while, some soldiers came to the Aquino house and gave all of his belongings to Cory. She didn't know if this meant he was alive or dead, and the soldiers refused to tell her. So, carrying her youngest baby, daughter Kris, she set out to visit nearly all of the Philippine prison camps, a pilgrimage of forty-three days. At each prison, the men in charge made Cory sit outside with the baby, regardless of whether it was raining or sunny. Many times she sat for hours, waiting for someone to tell her whether her husband was there.

Finally, she found him in Camp Laur, where he had been placed in solitary confinement. They had taken away his clothes and his eyeglasses, and had refused to let him have books to read. Deprived of all social contact, the outgoing and talkative Ninoy paced his tiny cell, reliving every event of his childhood in an attempt to keep from going crazy. At one point, he had a religious experience that he later said gave him faith. Until that point, he had always teased his wife about her religious devotion. Ninoy's new belief in God helped to bring him closer to Cory and his children.

It was a shock for her to see him on the other side of the barbed-wire fence in the prison camp. The baby cried, and soon Ninoy, too, broke down. Cory remembers, "It was the first time I saw Ninoy no longer the confident man I had always known." After that, she never saw him in the same way. He would always carry that vulnerability.

Cory then successfully appealed to have Ninoy transferred to Fort Bonifacio, a military prison. After two years, she obtained permission to make conjugal visits, which meant she could spend the night. Each time she entered the prison compound, she was subjected to humiliating body searches. Inside his cell, Cory was nervous because of the surveillance cameras and hidden microphones. She kept saying, "Oh, no, Ninoy! What if somebody's filming this?" and he would answer, "Look, we are married. So what do you want to be worried about?" One friend had warned her that the mirror in her husband's cell could be a one-way viewing device, so they put a blanket over it.

Locked in the cell for the weekend, Cory and Ninoy had plenty of time to discuss politics. Cory refers to this period as her "political education with one of the best teachers in politics," for it was during these visits that Ninoy discussed his dreams of helping to unite the Filipino people and create a new era of democracy.

On Sundays, the entire family often visited Ninoy in his prison cell, where he held an impromptu Sunday school, giving the kids Bible lessons. At Christmas and Easter, all seven of them would sleep on mattresses on the stone floor of his jail cell. The peephole in the cell door, normally used by the guards to watch Ninoy, became the magic door through which the imaginary Christmas dwarf delivered gifts to the children.

Cory found that being in jail gave her husband the chance to really examine his actions. "When he was in Bonifacio, he was so caring. Before that, he was so busy trying to be popular that we just had to be relegated to the background. Now he felt he owed each of us something. He really tried his best to make up to us for whatever we had lacked before."

After a few years, Ninoy began wondering if people outside jail remembered him. He gave Cory messages to deliver to his followers. For five years, she served as his courier to the outside world, calling news conferences to deliver Ninoy's statements. The first time she had to speak in public she was very nervous, but then she found that, "like everything else, once you get the hang of it, then it's really no big deal."

Ninoy's ideas were later photocopied or mimeographed and distributed to members of the underground opposition. In the Philippines, this was the only alternative press. Cory's mother-in-law, Aurora Aquino, says, "Contact with newspaper people made Cory really sharp." One of Ninoy's sisters adds, "The prison years were when we really began to admire Cory."

In 1978, Marcos permitted opposition politicians to run for the National Assembly. Ninoy campaigned for his old Senate seat from his cell, coaching Cory as to how she should answer certain questions for him.

Cory was still uncomfortable speaking in public and somewhat relieved when three of her children, —seven-year-old Kris; Noynoy, her son; and Ballsy, the eldest daughter, pitched in. Kris, who is now a singer and entertainer in the Philippines, put her natural talents to use on her father's behalf at a very young age. She became one of the big draws at rallies for the anti-Marcos opposition, being so persuasive at times that even grown men could be seen shedding tears.

President Marcos and his wife Imelda criticized Cory and Ninoy for "exploiting" their children for political ends. Cory, in turn, said the kids would be happy to stop campaigning for their father if the Marcoses would let him out of jail so he could do it himself.

Since the National Assembly elections were the first to be held since martial law was imposed, Marcos and his wife did not want to lose. Imelda Marcos was running for twenty-one political offices! Election "specialists" stuffed ballot boxes with phony ballots for the Marcos ticket, and voter registration lists were falsified.

"Vote early and vote often," a joke sometimes made about elections in other countries, was certainly true in the Philippines, where people who had been long dead voted for President Marcos's ruling party. People were paid to vote, and beaten up if they didn't. It was, if nothing else, a rehearsal for the presidential campaign of 1985–86, except that in 1978 Imelda Marcos won everything. For years to come, she was considered the person most likely to succeed her husband as head of state.

Despite Imelda's victory, support for Ninoy continued to grow. From his prison cell, through the voices of Cory and his children, Ninoy continued to criticize the Marcos regime. "The rule of the few has been eliminated," he once said. "It has been reduced to the rule of one."

Ninoy's detention also focused Cory's opposition to the Marcos regime. It was during this time that she developed her own political views, and in this sense her experience was similar to that of other wives of political prisoners: Winnie Mandela, whose husband, black opposition leader Nelson, has been jailed for twenty-two years for opposing South Africa's apartheid system of enforced segregation; Yelena Bonner, who shared internal exile with her dissident husband, Andrei Sakharov, because of his outspoken views on Soviet repression; and Isabel Letelier, widow of the Chilean ambassador who was assassinated in Washington, D.C., in 1976 for his opposition to the Chilean military regime that had earlier imprisoned him in a concentration camp near Antarctica. As a result of their husbands' imprisonment, Winnie Mandela, Elena Bonner, Isabel Letelier, and Corazon Aquino all developed strong views of their own about their respective governments, and all became fighters in their own right for the cause of freedom.

Detaining Ninoy Aquino began to have the opposite effect from the one Marcos originally intended. Instead of isolating his rival, imprisonment was helping to make Aquino better known and more popular than ever. So, Marcos sentenced Ninoy to death. The trumped-up charges against Aquino ranged from murder and arson to possession of illegal weapons. Ninoy went on a hunger strike for forty days. Cory helped him survive by smuggling vitamins in to him in a thermos. By the thirty-eighth day, he said that he thought he would die. On the fortieth day he was taken to the hospital, emaciated and dehydrated, with his skin hanging on him "like the stench of death," according to someone who saw him.

In 1980, while his sentence was under review by the Supreme Court, a judicial body packed with Marcos cronies, Ninoy suffered a major heart attack. He was taken from jail to the Philippine Heart Center in Manila.

Doctors there determined that he needed triple-bypass heart surgery. Aquino appealed to President Marcos to be allowed to go to the United States for medical treatment. Marcos said yes that same day.

The next morning, Imelda Marcos and Major General Fabian Ver, chief of staff of the Philippine armed forces, came to the hospital to help Ninoy leave by completing the necessary paperwork and providing him and his family with exit visas.

Despite all that Marcos had done to him, Ninoy Aquino was forgiving. He gave Mrs. Marcos a golden crucifix on a chain and said he wanted President Marcos to have it, since it had been his own good luck charm for seven years. Giving away his crucifix turned out to be the last act Benigno Aquino, Jr., would ever perform in his own country. But it would be years before anyone realized it.

Ninoy left two of his children for a period in Manila as a show of faith that he intended to return.

These two children joined him later. Cory and their three other children accompanied him, first to Dallas where he underwent surgery, and then to Cambridge, Massachusetts, where he accepted fellowships at M.I.T. and Harvard.

F I V E

Exile and Return

The Aquino children refer to their time in Boston as "the three years of togetherness." The family settled comfortably into a house in Newton, Massachusetts, a suburb of Boston. The house was close to Boston College, where daughter Victoria Elisa (Viel) was a student.

Corazon Aquino remembers it as the happiest time of her life. Her family was settled, and she was able to go back to being a housewife. She had time for her hobbies—growing miniature Japanese trees, called *bonsai,* and cooking gourmet meals. She even had a separate oven in which to cook her specialty, Peking duck—Ninoy's favorite.

After the stressful years of visiting Ninoy in prison every weekend, Cory finally found time to relax. She enjoyed watching American TV, which had not existed when she was a schoolgirl in Philadelphia. The entire family enjoyed watching soap operas on TV, but Cory's favorite show was "The $25,000 Pyramid."

There was time to read novels again, and time to write. Ninoy had been urging her to write ever since his detention, and now she began writing *haiku*, short Japanese-style poems. One of her favorites, in English, was this one:

> The worst of my life is over,
>   I hope,
> And may the best things, please,
>   come soon.

When Ninoy read it, he said that he thought there would be more bad times ahead. Cory didn't allow herself to think that way. They had already survived his imprisonment, his hunger strike, and his heart attack. What more could happen?

She determined to enjoy living in the present as fully as possible. And she seemed to slip back into her earlier passive role as Ninoy's wife. One friend remembers, "She played the role of companion to her husband. She was in the background all the time. I never heard her express her own political view. When I talked politics with Ninoy, Cory was sitting on the side, smiling."

But she was not entirely the same docile housewife she had been years ago. After one dinner, when someone suggested that the ladies leave so that the men could enjoy their cigars, Cory insisted she wanted to stay, since she was involved in the conversation.

It was harder for her to maintain a private home life, however. An innately political and social man, Ninoy kept inviting people to visit. And once again, as she had years earlier in Concepción, Cory found herself in a houseful of people she didn't know. It was tiring and irritating. Finally she asked Ninoy to stop inviting so many people. She said she needed to rest. And, she told him, there were some people she simply didn't like and did not want in her home. Ninoy's view of the scene was different. He told Cory not to be so transparent about her feelings. His was a politician's perspective.

Boston had given Ninoy a new life, and he took great pleasure in simply going to work. After seven years in jail, even taking a walk or driving a car was special to him. So was the time he had with his family. Ninoy and Ballsy, his oldest daughter, started going to warehouse sales. They enjoyed rummaging for bargains together. He helped her plan her wedding to a young man in the Philippines.

But family life wasn't all peaceful. Viel, the Aquinos' fourth daughter, still felt the effects of her father's years in prison, and she was worried about him. She wanted him to get out of politics entirely and become a Harvard professor. "Dad's great, and it's an honor," she said. "But given a choice, I'd rather have an ordinary father."

Tension between Ninoy and his only son, Noynoy, then twenty, mounted steadily. Noynoy had been twelve years old when his father was sent to jail. Ninoy told him he would have to be the man in the family. But he did poorly in high school and disappointed his father, who once wrote to him, "The only thing I will be leaving you is a name I have tried to keep clean and honest."

After graduating from college in the Philippines, Noynoy rejoined the family in Boston. But he couldn't figure out what he wanted to do and so he did nothing. It was a way of rebelling, of getting back at his energetic father. The two of them locked horns.

Noynoy then realized that in addition to his father's good name, he had grown up with more privileges than the average Filipino boy. He thought back to an incident when he was young, when he saw a boy selling newspapers on the street in Manila. He asked his mother why that boy didn't have to go to school, and she explained that the boy could not afford to go to school because he had to help support his family by selling papers. Remembering that, Noynoy decided to start his own business and turn it over to his employees once it became profitable. Then he'd be able to show his father how he had succeeded. In fact, the events that were to take place prevented him from doing this.

Meanwhile, Ninoy was being swept back into the political life of the Philippines and, more and more, he spoke about returning home. Although he no longer wanted to run for president, Ninoy Aquino did want to be active in the movement for a return to democracy in the Philippines. He wanted to organize the anti-Marcos opposition in preparation for the National Assembly elections in 1984. He announced that he had to go home "to prove to the Filipinos that I am not afraid, because I know they respect courage more than anything else." Besides, he added, "It is time for every Filipino living abroad who loves his country to return home and suffer with his people." One of Ninoy's associates at Harvard called his return "suicidal"—a word that proved sadly prophetic.

Newspaper columnist Jack Anderson believed that Ninoy chose to return because he had heard reports that Marcos was seriously ill. Marcos was reported to be suffering from a severe kidney disease, although he continually denied it.

Nicknamed "the Iron Butterfly," Imelda Marcos had her own eye on the Philippines' highest office. Some people say that's why she came to New York in May 1983 to warn Ninoy Aquino that he might be assassinated if he returned.

But Ninoy stuck to his guns. He began sending his books home to Manila, saying he would need them when he was sent back to jail for his nonviolent campaign against the Marcos regime.

On August 2, 1983, Defense Minister Juan Ponce Enrile telexed Ninoy, asking him not to return for at least a month because he was "convinced beyond a reasonable doubt that there are plots against your life upon your arrival in the Philippines." Ninoy decided to delay going back for two weeks to give the government a chance to catch anyone plotting to kill him.

Cory took it philosophically. "I knew we couldn't stay permanently in the United States," she says, adding that Ninoy "felt that three years was long enough to be away. Besides, what he had gone for, he had already accomplished."

On August 12, 1983, the night before he left Boston, Ninoy Aquino told a reporter, "This is a second life I can give up. Besides, if they shoot me, they'll make me a hero."

Cory cooked Ninoy's favorite dish, Peking duck, but after dinner neither of them could get to sleep. Cory felt cold, although it was August. She told her husband, "This is exactly how I felt after you were arrested, the day of martial law."

"Oh, let's not talk about it," Ninoy replied. "I told you long ago this is what we have to do."

"Yes," Cory said, "I just wanted to let you know how I felt."

The next morning, the entire Aquino family went to mass, and then many people dropped in to say good-bye. At the airport, Ninoy used a false passport from a Muslim country. Imelda Marcos had promised to provide him with a new Philippine passport after his old one expired, but she had never done so. Instead, Benigno Aquino, Jr., traveled under the name Marcial Bonifacio, a play on the term "martial law" and on the name of the prison in which he had spent so many years, Fort Bonifacio.

Cory's last words before he boarded his plane were, "Just call me at every stop." That way she would know everything was going according to schedule.

He phoned her from Los Angeles and later from Tokyo. She was busy packing, since she and the children planned to join him in Manila two weeks later. Ninoy had suggested that she might want to stay in Boston, but Cory wanted to keep the family together.

From Taipei, Ninoy phoned his family for the last

time. He had found it hard to go to sleep and spent much of the night saying the rosary. Cory read a passage from the Bible over the phone. As he spoke to each of the children, he began to cry. After he hung up, he wrote each of them a letter.

As he prepared to board China Airlines flight 811 for Manila on Sunday, August 21, 1983, Ninoy was greeted by two Chinese officials. One of them said they had received a phone call from Philippine Airlines in Manila and had been told to take good care of him. Ninoy's brother-in-law, ABC News correspondent Ken Kashiwahara was traveling with him. Aquino told him that the phone call meant that Marcos's men knew who he was, despite his alias.

At Manila airport, a crowd of about twenty thousand people gathered. Busloads of supporters, family members, and friends showed up, many wearing yellow and carrying yellow ribbons. The song "Tie a Yellow Ribbon 'round the Old Oak Tree" had come to symbolize the hope that Ninoy would return. About two thousand security men took up positions around the airport.

Aboard the plane, Ninoy Aquino chatted with reporters and fingered his rosary for much of the two-hour flight from Taiwan to Manila. He got up from seat 14C just before the plane landed and put on his bulletproof vest. He knew he'd be safe unless they hit him in the head. In that case, Ninoy had told his brother-in-law, "I'm a goner." He then handed Kashiwahara his gold watch, saying, "I just want you to have it." Believing that he would be taken directly to prison, Ninoy instructed Kashiwahara to go to his house and take his belongings to the jail. Kashiwahara smiled as the plane landed. "Ninoy, we're home."

When the plane's engine was turned off, three men wearing aviation security badges came into the cabin. One of them shook Ninoy's hand and called him "boss" in Tagalog, the unofficial native tongue of the Philippines.

Ninoy got out of his seat. One of the security men took his bag, and another held him by the arm to escort him down the aisle. Kashiwahara tried to accompany him, but a security man wearing sunglasses told him to get back in his seat. Ninoy, who had been smiling, suddenly looked grim.

A door leading to a boarding ramp was opened. Two television crews followed close behind as Ninoy was led to the door. Two plainclothesmen and two uniformed security officers stood nearby. As Ninoy stepped off the plane to get his first breath of Philippine air in three years, one shot rang out. People on the plane rushed to the door, only to be barred by security men.

Just outside the door, Benigno Aquino, Jr., pitched forward and fell to the ground, dead.

The Widow

In Boston, Corazon Aquino sensed something was wrong, and she was unable to sleep. "I was waiting for his call," she remembers. "It was past midnight. Then Ballsy, our eldest, came into my room and I asked why. She said, 'I can't sleep either.' It was then just one o'clock. I went to the bathroom; then I decided to pray the rosary. Later, taking account of the twelve-hour time difference between Boston and Manila, I realized that it was then, between one-ten and one-fifteen, that he was shot."

The first phone call about the shooting came in around two-thirty in the morning. Ballsy answered the phone. A reporter from a Japanese news agency in New York said that someone had been shot in Manila.

"They think it's Dad, and they want to know if we've heard," Ballsy told her mother, who immediately came to the phone.

"We have heard from Tokyo that your husband has been shot," the reporter told Corazon Aquino.

"Are you sure?" she asked.

"Yes."

Another call, this one from a friend in Japan, soon confirmed the tragic news. A Japanese reporter who had been on the plane with Ninoy had seen him shot in the head.

Cory gathered her children together and told them about the report that their father was dead, adding that she hoped it was just a rumor. Everyone gathered in the attic to watch the news reports on T.V. Kris, the youngest, had been asleep in her mother's bedroom, but they woke her to tell her what had happened.

Everyone was sitting around the TV crying, waiting for the reports to come in. Cory thought it would help calm the children down if everyone prayed together, so they did. Then, at 6:00 A.M., they all went to mass. Friends came by later to offer support.

All this time, Cory kept an ear cocked for the phone to ring. She expected a call from her family in Manila and was troubled when it didn't come. Finally she realized, "They didn't know how to tell me; they didn't know how to break it to me. They were still hoping it was just a rumor." The phone call came much later, after her family in Manila was sure that Cory already knew.

It was a bitter homecoming for the Aquino family. Instead of rejoining Ninoy, they returned to Manila to cope with his death. Noynoy called it "the last crisis in a series of crises."

But they were not prepared for the mass outpouring of grief and love that awaited them. More than one million people lined the 100-mile route along which the old hearse carried Aquino's body to the cathedral in Manila. The hearse inched its way through crowds of people chanting, "Ninoy, Ninoy, Ninoy!"

More than seventy-five thousand people flocked around a church near Clark Air Force Base as the hearse passed through the area. And when it finally arrived at the cathedral, another half-million turned out to pay their respects.

One reporter described it as "the largest demonstration of public emotion in Philippine history." But it was far surpassed several days later when twice as many people showed up for the funeral.

The 13-mile journey from the cathedral to the cemetery, which normally took forty minutes, took

Corazon Aquino and son Noy at Ninoy's coffin. Tarlac province, July 29, 1983.

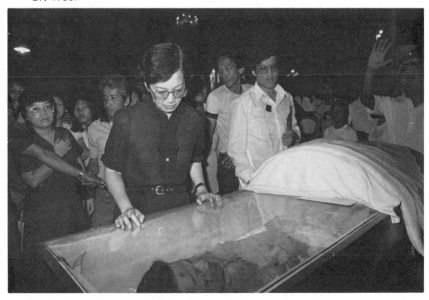

eleven hours on that sad day. Mourners chanted, "Ninoy, Ninoy!" and carried signs proclaiming, "Marcos is a killer," and, "Marcos the Great Liar."

The night after Aquino was buried, hundreds of people stormed Malacanang Palace where the Marcoses lived. They threw rocks and bottles. Riot police fought back. By morning, one protester had been killed and seventy-four other people injured.

It was one of the most violent outbursts against Marcos in ten years, indicating that public confidence in his regime was disintegrating.

Marcos called Aquino's murder "a heinous crime" and appointed a commission of his own supporters to investigate it. He accused the communist insurgents, known as the National People's Army (NPA), of having hired a killer to gun down Aquino, calling his death "a communist rubout." But his explanations fell on deaf ears; most Filipinos believed that Marcos himself had ordered Aquino murdered.

One Filipino reporter, however, claimed that he didn't think Marcos had planned the killing. He thought Imelda was behind the murder. With Aquino out of the way, she believed she would have a clear path to succeed her husband. The Filipino reporter was present in the palace when Marcos learned about the airport assassination. Apparently, the Philippine leader was so furious that he threw things at his assistants. It appears that he was smart enough to realize that Aquino dead would be a more potent enemy than Aquino alive.

All too soon, that proved to be true. Aquino's funeral had turned into a political event, and more big anti-Marcos protests followed. Even President Reagan was forced to reconsider his attitude toward the Philippines. Until now, the Reagan administration had been a strong supporter of Ferdinand Marcos, overlooking his authoritarian excesses because of his strong anti-communist position. On an official trip to Manila in 1981, Vice President George Bush had toasted Marcos, saying, "We love your adherence to democratic principles and to the democratic processes."

But now, two years later, there was no way Mr. Reagan could ignore the signals from Manila. He decided to cancel a scheduled trip to Manila, a gesture which indicated that now, he, too, was losing confidence in Marcos's ability to govern. Added to that, the Philippine economy hit an all-time low as a result of the political turbulence.

The investigation into Aquino's death got off to a bad start. Public confidence in the investigating team was low to begin with. It fell even lower after investigators identified Aquino's murderer as a gun-for-hire named Rolando Galman who worked for criminal syndicates and communist subversives. Galman had been shot dead seconds after Aquino. His body, wearing the uniform of an aviation mechanic, lay on the tarmac just yards from Ninoy's.

Galman's family came to claim his body and asked the five-member investigating commission to grant them protection. But no action was taken, and Galman's mother and sister were soon kidnapped by unidentified gunmen. Later it was revealed that Galman's mother had been kidnapped by the Philippine Air Force for undisclosed reasons. The abductions seemed geared toward discouraging potential witnesses, especially those who had seen anything different from what the government investigators wanted to be seen.

Filipinos talked about nothing but the Aquino murder, and they had many doubts, including one important question: Was Galman really the killer? A Japanese reporter, who had been on the plane, said that Galman had actually been standing in front of Aquino, not behind him. And he was not carrying a weapon. It was possible that Galman had been pushed onto the runway and shot so that he would appear to have been Aquino's murderer. Some people said that Aquino had actually been shot by someone standing above him, possibly one of the aviation security men who had escorted him out of the airplane.

A Japanese photographer had snapped some pictures showing a man in a presidential security uniform looking out from behind a luggage cart and then running away. Perhaps he had shot Galman to make it look as though Galman shot Aquino.

And people around the world were asking how any murderer could have gotten so close to Aquino when the Marcos government knew that people were plotting to murder him. How could the security men have been so careless? And why didn't the two thousand airport security men take any action to protect Aquino? Perhaps they were just there to make it look as though the government was concerned for Aquino's safety.

With so many questions unanswered and so few

people believing the official version, Marcos appointed a civilian commission headed by Justice Corazon Agrava to conduct yet another investigation into the killing.

The Agrava Commission worked on the case from November 1983 until August 1984, examining 1,294 documents, 1,472 photographs, and 14 videotapes. During the 125 public hearings, 91 pieces of physical evidence were introduced and 193 witnesses testified. In the end, the commission generated a 20,377-page transcript.

On October 23, 1984, Justice Agrava went alone to see President Marcos. Their meeting was broadcast on Philippine television. She handed him a report that she had written. In it, she said that General Luthero Custodio, the former chief of aviation security, and six of his employees were responsible for killing Aquino.

The next day, the other members of the commission presented their report, naming several officers of the Philippine armed forces as responsible for Aquino's death. Some of the officers were generals. One of them was Major General Fabian Ver, chief of staff of the armed forces and a major ally of Marcos.

According to this new report, Galman had shot Aquino, but he had in fact been a puppet of those who had planned the killing. The evidence indicated that Galman had no motive for killing Benigno Aquino and that it would have been impossible for him to have shot Aquino without the aid of others. The commission claimed that military authorities knew when Aquino would arrive at the Manila airport and created a huge cover-up operation to make it look as though they were trying to protect his life. The commission report ridiculed Marcos's contention that communists had killed Aquino, calling that simply absurd.

Corazon Aquino refused to participate in the investigation. She claimed that justice would never be done as long as Ferdinand Marcos was in power. Nor was she impatient for results. "After all, whether we have a real court of justice now or later, that will not bring Ninoy back to me," she said.

But there was another, more important reason why she was holding back and waiting. Justice, she believed, was not something that should be reserved for her. Rather, it was due to all of Marcos's victims.

It was about this time, while the commission was investigating her husband's murder, that Corazon Aquino began to develop her own political identity. Although she was often compared to President Kennedy's widow, Cory did not retreat into private life as Jacqueline Kennedy did. Instead, Cory began to address rallies, speaking softly to the crowds.

"I know none of you believe that Rolando Galman killed my husband," she would begin. "I believe he was shot by a soldier. But what I want to know is this—who ordered the killing?"

A low murmur from the crowd would grow to a rumble. "Marcos, Marcos."

Corazon Aquino was on her way.

SEVEN

The Candidate

"I am just one of the thousands and millions of victims of the Marcos regime," Cory would tell the crowds who came to hear her speak. "I am not the victim who has suffered the most, but perhaps the victim who is best known. I look around me and I see a nation that is sinking deeper and deeper into despair. I sense a growing feeling of helplessness and a creeping belief that no matter what abuse may be thrown at our faces, we are powerless to do anything about it." And since the Philippines needed an "unequivocal change" from the twenty-year rule of Ferdinand Marcos, she announced on December 3, 1985, that she would run against him for the presidency.

"I plan to seek justice not only for Ninoy but for all the victims of Marcos," she said, when asked to state her main reason for deciding to run.

Her decision came one day after three judges appointed by Marcos had acquitted Major General Ver and the other officers in the conspiracy to murder her husband, an action that outraged even the head of the normally conservative Philippine Roman Catholic church, Jaime Cardinal Sin.

"It threatens to push our country to the brink of despair," said Cardinal Sin. "It seems that an historic opportunity to restore the credibility of government and to satisfy our people's aspirations for truth and justice was lost."

Although Corazon Aquino's decision to challenge Marcos was well timed, making that decision had torn her apart. She did not initially want to run for president, but politics had become an increasingly important part of her life since Ninoy's death.

During the spring following his assassination, Cory had become a voice for change. She had campaigned for opposition candidates who were running against Marcos-backed contenders for seats in the National Assembly. More and more often, she was asked to become a spokesman for the factions opposed to Marcos. And, partly because of public anger over Ninoy's murder, the opposition won a larger share of the vote than anyone expected in those violent elections, gaining forty-three out of two hundred seats. Although forty-three out of two hundred did not appear to be a large victory, in the context of the Marcos-dominated legislature, it marked a significant gain for the opposition.

It was also during this campaign that Cory emerged as a strong individual in her own right. For years, she had been telling herself that she existed only as Ninoy's wife and that she herself knew little or nothing about politics. But more and more she found herself listening to advisers and realizing that she knew more than they did. On the one hand, they looked up to her as the head of the anti-Marcos movement. On the other hand, they kept telling her what to do, insisting that they knew better. One day, she had enough. "If I'm so important, why can't I do it the way I want to?" she demanded, with more emotion than anyone had ever seen her display. "I'm saying good-bye to all of you."

Her advisers did an about-face. "We're sorry we did not see it your way."

One year later, Cory still insisted, "I was amazed at myself." Her strength continued to grow. People from different groups opposed to Marcos kept asking for Cory's endorsement on their brochures, banners, protests, and other political projects. "Every candidate insists my words will make the difference between their winning and losing," she said. "I have to do what I can, but I look forward every night to the privacy of my room, to my time alone." But privacy became more and more elusive as Cory went from group to group with her appeal: "Please unite, because if we don't show any unity this early, all may be lost."

Marcos hoped she would fail. He wanted to face as many opposition parties as possible—"the more the merrier," he commented. He underestimated Corazon Aquino and refused to take her seriously, even when she managed to accomplish what her husband Ninoy had been unable to do: She united the many opposition groups into one.

Cory's strongest appeal as a candidate was in her morality, which contrasted dramatically with the immorality of the power-hungry rulers. "The only thing I can offer the Filipino people is my sincerity," she said. "They are fed up with people who keep promising them so many things and not being able to fulfill these promises." She maintained, "I cannot promise you anything because it would be dishonest of me to promise you that a better life will be there a week, a month, or even a year after I have been in office."

She did promise that she would put Marcos on trial for the murder of her husband, calling him the number one suspect. "I will file charges against him." She later changed that to "Maybe I will be one of many. Maybe it doesn't even have to be me." She insisted, however, that Marcos could remain politically active, despite criticism from members of her own party. "Why not?" she answered them. "My goodness, if I want to bring back democracy to this country, I'd be the last person to object."

The need for a strong democracy was urgent, not only because of the abuses of the Marcos regime but also because the communists were growing stronger. Cory believed that a strong non-communist opposition would upset their timetable for overthrowing the government. The communists "were hoping that Marcos would still be very much in control, that the people would not be awakened, and that when things were really bad, the only choice left would be the communists," Cory said.

Despite her popularity, her growing self-confidence, and her belief that she knew what her country needed, Corazon Aquino still did not really want to run for president. She kept hoping that the opposition would unite behind somebody else, and she prayed to be sure that seeking office was the right thing to do. Her children prayed, "Dear God, help us to accept your will but please let it not be our mother." On several nights, she had a dream in which she saw Ninoy's coffin, but when she got up close to it, she saw that it was empty. She interpreted the dream to mean that Ninoy, the soul of opposition to Marcos, was now part of her.

Finally, she requested that a petition be distributed for signatures. If one million people signed to support her candidacy, she would consider entering the race for president.

On December 1, a crowd of fifteen thousand people gathered outside a Manila cathedral. "You will hear what you want to hear," Corazon Aquino told them. The crowd cheered, "Long live President Cory Aquino," and waved banners saying, "Cory Aquino for President." Inside the cathedral, a priest sprinkled holy water on the signatures, all 1,200,286 of them.

Two days later, Corazon Aquino filled in an official certificate of candidacy for the office of president. In the space marked "occupation," she wrote "housewife," but she explained, "I am not a housewife anymore because I cannot take care of my house anymore. So many things have come up."

Her children were upset, and asked, "Mom, haven't you done enough?"

She told them, "Apparently in this world you can't say at a certain point, 'Okay, I've done my quota of suffering and no more.'"

Her running mate for the position of vice presi-

dent was former Senator, Salvador Laurel. He had
supported Marcos until 1982 when he broke away
and became the head of an opposition party, an
opposition party different from Benigno Aquino's.
Laurel had wanted to run for president himself,
hoping that Cory would agree to be the spiritual
inspiration of the campaign and allow him to be the
front runner.

Having made up her mind, though, Cory was
determined to run. She shrewdly handled the back-
room bargaining, arguing that unless they came up
with one ticket, Marcos would win, because the two
opposition candidates would take votes away from
each other. Laurel deferred to her greater personal
following and agreed to accept the number two
spot on the ticket.

"To pave the way for the holding of a special
election for president, I hereby irrevocably vacate
the position of president," Marcos wrote in a letter
to the National Assembly on November 8, 1985.
Actually, his second constitutional term had ex-

"Co-ry! Co-ry!" Corazon Aquino campaigns for the Presidency.
January 3, 1986.

pired in 1973, but he had long since rewritten the constitution to extend his term of office indefinitely.

That's why no one could quite believe it when he called for elections. Of course, there were plenty of reasons for Marcos to feel insecure enough to want to hold elections: his growing unpopularity in the wake of the Aquino assassination, for one. For another, the communist insurgents were gaining strongholds on some of the smaller islands. And that made the Reagan administration nervous.

A number of officials from the United States had "dropped in" on Malacanang Palace to lecture Marcos on his failings. Marcos kept promising to be more democratic, but he went right on being a dictator, because he did not believe the officials were speaking for President Reagan. That changed, however, when President Reagan sent his friend Senator Paul Laxalt to Manila. Shortly after Laxalt's visit, Ferdinand Marcos called for presidential elections.

Of course, Marcos did not expect to lose. After all, he had ruled for twenty years and he believed the majority of the Philippine people supported him. In any case, he had full use of the military and his own private brigades to make sure that people voted for him. He had his election specialists schooled in the art of making sure that no one on the Marcos ticket, especially the leader himself, ever lost an election. Without a doubt, he believed he would be swept back into office, thereby silencing his critics.

Marcos once wrote that he wished to be remembered as a thinker, but it is more likely he will be remembered as a dictator. Many observers have pointed to strong similarities between Marcos and the late Shah of Iran. Like the shah, Marcos was an authoritarian ruler of a poor country who had strengthened the military and enriched his friends and family while imposing harsh measures on his subjects in order to stifle dissent. Also, like the shah, Marcos had long governed by his own will instead of by the will of the people. Nonetheless, all the tricks in his dictator's bag had failed to kill his people's desire for truth and freedom.

Marcos believed he had all the time in the world. After he won, he said, he would begin to reform. "We are going to reform the whole government," he promised. He said that he might even rewrite the constitution again, abolishing his own right to issue decrees without the approval of the National Assembly. One U.S. senator listened to Marcos carefully, then asked seven Filipino businessmen whether they thought Marcos would change after the election. "Forget it," all seven replied.

The two candidates never met face to face, and Marcos refused to debate Aquino on television, claiming that there was "nothing to debate." Nevertheless, the campaign had the flavor of a showdown in the Wild West. Aquino dared Marcos to debate her on TV, taunting, "And may the better woman win!" It was no holds barred all the way.

"In these times of crisis, what this country needs is a man! A bull! A stud! Vote Marcos, Marcos, Marcos!" a woman's voice shouted from a campaign van cruising the streets of Manila. Marcos supporters carried banners with the slogan "Tested in Crisis." Aquino, they said, was "Tested in House-wifery." Marcos borrowed a couple of slogans from former U.S. campaigns. Crowds chanted "Marcos's the one," and his billboards and bumper stickers read, "Now More Than Ever." Those slogans had been used in 1972 by President Nixon, who was later forced to resign from office.

Marcos confessed he found it demeaning to run against a woman. "It makes me feel small," he said. "I was taught by my father early in life never to argue with a woman, never lift a hand against a woman. The Filipino woman should be intelligent but demure. She can run her husband, but she should run him through the bedroom."

Aquino counterattacked: "Sure, I don't know anything about stealing or cheating, and definitely I don't know anything about killing my opponents."

President Ferdinand Marcos with young supporter during Presidential campaign. January 1986.

She went even further. When Marcos threatened to bring back military rule, she said, "Let him get a gun and come and shoot me." Imelda Marcos got into the act, too. Known for her extravagant clothes and jewelry, Imelda criticized Corazon Aquino for wearing yellow, the color that had become the symbol of the opposition. "Thank God, my skin looks good in many colors," Imelda said, adding that she didn't like yellow because it reminded her of "a lemon and jaundice." Cory remarked that it was revealing that Imelda had nothing better to do than comment on her wardrobe, in a country where "millions are unemployed, where millions are hungry." She said it was too bad that Imelda "never realized what her obligations were."

Imelda was energetically campaigning for her husband's vice-presidential candidate, Arturo Tolentino. Some officials nicknamed Tolentino "Jukebox" because "you put your money in and get the

Imelda Marcos with visiting Vietnamese dignitary.

President Ferdinand Marcos holds microphone for Imelda Marcos.

tune you want to hear." Even though Marcos had fired Tolentino from the post of foreign minister the year before, he now wanted him for a running mate. Tolentino was easy to control, and many people believed he would be just a figurehead. It was actually Imelda who was running for office.

That's what it looked like at Tolentino's campaign rallies. The candidate would give a speech then stand back as Imelda took over, singing American songs. One of her favorites was "Deep in the Heart of Texas." Another was "Don't Fence Me In." If her husband—whom she called "Marcos"—was there, they would sing duets.

Marcos himself didn't campaign much, preferring to spend more time at the palace lifting weights and doing his exercises. "The old man is a health freak," said Marcos's twenty-three-year-old son Ferdinand Junior, known as Bongbong. Imelda said her only form of exercise was "keeping a clear conscience."

Corazon Aquino never sang to the crowds, but sometimes her daughter Kris did. During the 1978 race, the Aquino children had campaigned for their father; now they stumped for their mother. Ballsy, the eldest, coordinated the campaign from Manila. Viel canvassed voters from door to door, since she disliked speaking in public. Noynoy and Kris worked the crowds. Sometimes Kris had a touch of stage fright. She would then just look at her mother, the candidate, and smile. The crowds loved it.

And they loved Cory. In one small town, ten thousand people waited for six hours in the rain to hear her speak. When she did, they cheered and applauded so much that she could hardly be heard. On February 5, one million people turned out for a rally, chanting, "Co-ry! Co-ry!" throughout her speech.

But it wasn't always the big crowds that demanded Cory's attention. One afternoon, while her campaign van was caught in a traffic jam, a group of boys ran over and stuck their hands through the open window, asking for campaign buttons. Cory found a few, but not enough to go around. The boys started yelling, and one of them pointed out that she had passed through the same neighborhood the day before and had given out some of the buttons, and one of the boys had gotten buttons on both days. It wasn't fair, they said. Cory spent a long time talking to the group about being fair and the rights of others. Eventually, they stopped shouting and dispersed peacefully. A passenger in the van observed that Cory didn't think it was beneath her to help settle their dispute.

Corazon Aquino campaigns for President.

At first, the world was stunned by the campaign. Nobody had expected Marcos to call elections. When he did, nobody expected Cory to run. And when she did, nobody expected her to win. But as the campaign progressed, and millions of people took to the streets to support her in a show of what she called "people power," the world took notice, and people everywhere began to believe that perhaps the impossible could happen. Aware that Philippine-style elections were nothing like those in America, the United States sent a team of independent observers to the Philippines to observe the elections. Senator Richard Lugar, chairman of the Foreign Relations Committee, headed the team.

The Americans had reason to be wary, not just

because of Marcos's past practices but also because the presidential campaign had been marred by violence. Two of Aquino's campaign organizers were killed by unidentified gunmen believed to be Marcos supporters. One of the victims was Cory's godson. "I ask Mr. Marcos to look into this and stop these killings," Aquino said. "I hold him responsible for any killings of my political leaders."

The U.S. observers also feared some last-minute trick by Marcos to steal the election in the event that voting did not go his way. A joke going around Manila told of how President Reagan, Soviet leader Gorbachev, and Ferdinand Marcos were all traveling in a plane that was about to crash. They had only one parachute among them. President Reagan said the parachute should be his because he was the leader of the free world. Gorbachev claimed it as head of the communist bloc. Marcos called for a vote, counted the ballots, and declared himself the winner 14 to 2.

"Today we are near the end of the first stage of our journey, a journey that began on the tarmac of the Manila airport in 1983. From that dark moment we have arrived at the dawn of a new Philippines. The people have spoken as never before." With those words, Corazon Aquino wrapped up her campaign on the night of February 6, 1986.

The next day at 7:00 A.M., millions of voters began arriving at polling stations throughout the Philippines. Voting ended at 3:00 P.M. Ferdinand Marcos declared the elections generally clean and said that if they proceeded as he expected, he and Tolentino would win all seventy-three provinces. An independent Philippine observer group, however, condemned the electoral process, claiming that there had been ten times more "cheating, fraud, intimidation, and harassment" than in the 1984 elections. Armed thugs sent by the Marcos team tried to steal ballot boxes from some polling places, but people threw themselves onto those boxes to prevent them from being taken. More than thirteen people were killed and seven wounded in campaign-related violence.

Corazon Aquino declared her victory the day after the elections. Senator Richard Lugar said that he was disturbed by the delay in counting the ballots.

There were, of course, two different vote counts. The Marcos-sponsored tally gave him a wide lead. But the independent Philippine vote-counting board said that Aquino was ahead. Aquino's party was afraid that Marcos would tamper with the results by sending forged ballots to the National Assembly for the final vote.

At the official vote-counting center, thirty vote counters walked out on Sunday, February 8. They said they were protesting the "deliberate changing of the election results coming directly from the precincts into the terminal they were manning."

Although Aquino held the lead in the independent vote tally, the National Assembly finished the "official" vote count and declared Marcos the winner by one and a half million votes.

On Sunday, February 23, 1986, several thousand Filipinos got down on their knees in the middle of a field. In front of them, a line of Philippine army tanks was revving up. From the tanks, a pro-Marcos soldier shouted through a bullhorn for the people to leave. The people refused. Instead, they recited the rosary and gave flowers to the troops.

The tanks turned back and headed back to the barracks instead of across the field where the human barricade was protecting the soldiers who had defected to the Aquino camp.

Such was the power of Corazon Aquino's continuing campaign. When it appeared that Marcos was cheating her of victory, she declared a campaign of nonviolence, going so far as to call for a general strike on February 25, the day of Marcos's inauguration. The Roman Catholic church, which had supported her run for office, backed her in this as well. Nuns and priests joined the protesters.

Effective though it was, the nonviolent campaign was not Marcos's greatest problem. His own top generals, Enrile and Ramos, defected to the Aquino camp. Ironically, General Enrile was the same man who used to grant or refuse Corazon Aquino's request to visit her husband in prison. Now Enrile and Ramos resigned from their posts and demanded that Marcos step down in favor of Aquino. The military split into armed factions, fighting each other in the streets.

The U.S. Congress and then President Reagan, charged Marcos and his supporters with widespread election abuse and called the election invalid. Marcos accused the United States of "foreign intervention." By the time President Reagan called on him to step down, Marcos knew the game was up.

Savoring her victory, Corazon Aquino called the elections "the most shameless in the world's living memory." She said, "Marcos pulled out all the stops . . . and did it all before the eyes of his own people and the world. Despite all this, I won."

E I G H T

The First One Hundred Days

"You people were so tolerant and so patient under Marcos for twenty years, and here I am only two days in office and you are expecting miracles. Then I talked to the nonviolent group, and again here come their protests, and I said, 'This is all the thanks I get? Here I am giving you my all and you people are still complaining. Why did I go through this exercise? You can get somebody else.'" President Corazon Aquino was learning the hard way, and learning quickly, that you simply can't please all the people all of the time. Even during the first few days of confrontations within her own party, thousands of people were still celebrating her victory in the streets.

Just two days earlier, she had stood before the nation claiming victory. "We are finally free, and we can be truly proud of the unprecedented way we achieved our freedom, with courage, with determination, and most important, in peace. A new life starts for our country."

But making that new life work was proving extremely difficult, as the woman in charge of what everyone called "the Cory government" rolled up her sleeves and got down to work.

Her first act after taking office was to appoint a presidential cabinet of seventeen advisers. All of them had been opposed to President Marcos. Thirteen of them were lawyers, and five had attended Harvard University or Yale. She was accused of making her cabinet too "elite," of not bringing in farmers and poor people. She was called "stubborn" for having made her selections by herself, without consulting different political factions. A professional politician would have bargained to have different groups represented, someone in her government said. Finally, she was blamed for having made poor choices. Someone sneered that Cory's cabinet was "made up of people you couldn't invite to a party together."

Whatever their individual differences, the cabinet members got right down to work, too. Their first project was figuring out how to run the government without having to abide by the structure set up by Ferdinand Marcos.

Keeping her campaign promise to release political prisoners, President Aquino freed 480 detainees during her first week in office. Under protest from the military, she then decided to free four communist leaders who had remained in jail, saying that this would help promote dialogue with the underground rebels.

Her government began a new investigation into Benigno Aquino's 1983 assassination. New witnesses suddenly came forward. With Marcos gone, they were now unafraid to testify. President Aquino announced that she would not extradite Marcos from Hawaii to face charges. "I can be magnanimous in victory," she said. "It is time to heal wounds and forget the past."

As during her campaign, she continued to work sixteen-hour days, driving herself to the limit. But now, as president, she suffered from terrible headaches. Her only enjoyment was having dinner with her family, including her baby grandson Justin Benigno. David Hartman of ABC's "Good Morning America," who interviewed President Aquino, said that he was impressed with her honesty and faith and that "she is today as committed to being a full-time parent as she is a full-time president." Her role as mother changed somewhat upon taking office: Instead of reminding her daughters to button up their sweaters, she now had to tell them not to go out without their security guards.

Five days after the new government took power, hundreds of thousands of people rallied to support it. "People power has brought down a dictator," Cory told the cheering crowd. But she warned that "the situation, while stable, is not totally under control yet." Civilians and troops loyal to Ferdinand Marcos were still a force to be reckoned with.

"The danger is not yet past," agreed Cardinal Sin. "We must continue to watch, work, and pray."

As her first proclamation, President Aquino announced she was restoring habeas corpus, a law that protects citizens against illegal arrest. Marcos had suspended it in 1981, although at the time he had lifted other provisions of "smiling martial law."

President Aquino also called for a continuation of the "people power" that had swept her into office, asking her supporters to form grass-roots organizations to participate in governing the country.

Vice President Salvador Laurel was angry at President Aquino for having called the rally without consulting him. President Aquino said to a friend that Laurel had forgotten that "*I'm* the one who ran for president."

Women, who had played such an important role in ridding the country of Marcos, turned out in Manila to thank President Aquino on International Women's Day, March 9. Carrying flowers, many of the five thousand women sported short hairdos like the new president's and wore glasses like hers. Aquino souvenirs sprouted from vendors' carts —everything from yellow T-shirts saying "People Power" to Cory dolls with eyeglasses, Cory key rings, pendants, hats, and lapel pins.

"It was the women who knelt in the path of oncoming tanks and called the bluff of the dictator," President Aquino told them. "And it is a woman who stands here before you today as the president of a new, free, and proud Philippines."

The crowd applauded. "We salute and honor you, Mrs. President, for giving us back our collective voices as women," someone said. "And for helping us get rid of the macho dictator," someone else piped up.

President Aquino stood before them smiling. "I know I can rely on you, my sisters."

In the days that followed, she named a human

rights committee to investigate the murder, torture, and disappearance of thousands of people during the Marcos regime. Her defense minister, Juan Enrile, announced that two of Ferdinand Marcos's secret police agencies would be phased out. Those agencies had also been responsible for human rights abuses, including widespread monitoring and arrest of civilians. As the committee began work, communist-led fighting intensified. More than one hundred people were killed as a result of it during the first three weeks that President Aquino was in office. Her efforts to secure a cease-fire, however, were considered by the military leaders to be counterproductive. The military believed that the communists would use the duration of the cease-fire to strengthen their positions.

In addition to communist insurgents, President Aquino inherited a Muslim rebellion in the southern part of the country. For the past seventeen years, Muslim forces had been fighting government troops. To keep channels open, President Aquino met with rebel leaders and negotiated a temporary cease-fire so talks could continue. But she did not

President Aquino at ceremony marking the third anniversary of Ninoy's death. August 21, 1986.

support the idea of a separate Muslim state, the rebels' apparent goal.

President Aquino's most popular actions centered on Malacanang Palace, the former official residence. In keeping with one of her original campaign promises, President Aquino refused to live there. This, despite urging from her daughter Kris to move in "because the bathrooms are like the ones on 'Dynasty.'" Instead, President Aquino moved her family and her offices into a small guest house on the palace grounds.

While setting up their offices, the members of the new government began investigating the Marcoses' foreign investments, said to be worth billions of dollars. This, too, was a campaign pledge fulfilled. (When Marcos and his group arrived in Honolulu on February 27, U.S. customs officials seized a crate containing one million dollars in cash, which the former ruler was trying to bring into the United States.) Ferdinand and Imelda Marcos had set up foundations to hide even more of the money they'd invested overseas. Among their holdings were several buildings in New York City, including a multilevel shopping center, and a few large estates furnished with expensive artwork, furniture, and antiques.

On March 14, President Aquino kept yet another promise: she opened the presidential palace to the public, and she made sure that poor people got a chance to enter first. Marcos had never allowed the public to enter the palace grounds.

Thousands of poor Filipinos lined up outside the palace gates early that morning, eager to see the legendary wealth that the Marcoses had acquired at the expense of the people. So many came that there was some pushing and shoving, and a few dozen people passed out in the 90-degree heat. President Aquino quieted the crowd, explaining, as people filed past, that when they saw what was inside they would understand why their country was in such a poor financial state.

Imelda Marcos's opulent bedroom in Malacanang Palace. March 1986.

Marcos's study contained a rack of rifles neatly stacked in case he should need them to fight back rebels. The guns looked as if they had never been touched. In a country lacking medical facilities, Marcos had enjoyed a private hospital filled with the latest equipment, including three dialysis machines. The machines proved that the rumors about Marcos's kidney disease had been true.

In the basement, Imelda's storerooms housed hundreds of designer gowns, all size eight, many still bearing their price tags. Some people started calling it "Imelda's department store." Upstairs in her opulent suite, Imelda's shoe collection was the main attraction. Initial reports from Malacanang Palace indicated that the former First Lady had acquired approximately 3,000 pairs of shoes. But nearly one year after their discovery, that figure was revised to 1,060.

A more complete inventory of Imelda's collections revealed that she had left behind 508 floor-length gowns, 427 dresses, 888 handbags, 464 scarves, 664 handkerchiefs, 71 pairs of sunglasses, 65 parasols, 15 mink coats, and one swan-feather gown—in addition to her shoes.

Imelda's extravagance with public money had long been common knowledge in the Philippines. According to one report, she had spent more than $2 million of public money on her daughter's wedding a few years back. One of Imelda's friends had imported $20,000 worth of flowers for the event. When they arrived, Imelda didn't like the color; she threw them out and ordered another $20,000 "bouquet." One of her wedding gifts to the bridal couple was the right to collect one dollar in duty on every bottle of wine imported into the Philippines.

From her home in exile in Hawaii, Imelda said, "I have no weakness for shoes. I wear very simple shoes, which are pumps." The 1,060 pairs of shoes in Malcanang Palace belonged to her daughters and to the palace employees, she says, even though all the shoes were the same size: 8½. Imelda insists she wore a size seven shoe until very recently and that she does not have as many pairs of shoes as the Aquino government claims she does.

She accused the Aquino government of making up stories to discredit her. She also charged the Aquino government with forging her signature on documents showing she spent $7 million on jewelry alone in 1983. The jewelry included a $100,000 necklace and a $208,000 bracelet. Her signature also was found on the papers for the Swiss bank accounts where she allegedly squirreled away hundreds of millions. Imelda denies she signed those, too. Actually, the entire value of the Marcos's Swiss bank accounts has been estimated at $5 billion.

Nowadays, Imelda is crying poverty, claiming she is forced to live in a "rental"—a waterfront home worth about $1 million—and she insists she has no idea how much money she has. "If you know how much you've got, you probably haven't got much," she says.

Corazon Aquino came from a very rich family, but Imelda's family was poor. She said that she decided to reach "for excellence, for life, for love and beauty and God" in the hope that this would somehow wipe out the bad memories of her childhood. But Imelda was unable to see that by satisfying her own desires she was hurting the people whom she and her husband governed.

Opening the palace confirmed millions of people's worst suspicions about the Marcoses. In addition to the furnishings and clothes, there were hundreds of videotapes showing the Marcos family living it up. Many showed Imelda dressed in expensive gowns, dripping with jewelry, singing to her guests.

In one of the tapes, taken on the presidential yacht, Ferdinand's and Imelda's son Bongbong is seen wearing a bow tie that lights up. He is crooning "We Are the World," the popular theme song of the worldwide campaign to help starving people in Ethiopia. It's unlikely that Bongbong or his parents got the message, since they did not have to look too far to see their own people rummaging through the garbage for food.

President Aquino's simple life-style was itself a reassurance to millions of poverty-stricken Filipinos. Despite her family wealth, they believed that she was the right leader for them because, as one said, "she is just like us." Her suffering had made her one of them.

But criticism of the new president heated up as she approached the end of her first hundred days in office. The new government was "like a child learning to walk," according to Cardinal Sin, one of its strongest supporters. Among their first stumbling steps, the new leaders somehow managed to appoint three different people for the same government job. Even Cory's supporters were dismayed.

They began to say she was "vague and indecisive" while she was trying to decide whether or not to disband the National Assembly, which was packed with Marcos loyalists. She also seemed unable to make up her mind to abolish the constitution, which Marcos had rewritten. One observer said she was being so timid that she seemed to have "slipped back into the housewife role."

When she did strike down the constitution, retaining the Bill of Rights to prevent abuse of power until a new constitution could be written, she was branded "a dictator like Marcos." President Aquino moved quickly to appoint a commission to draft a new constitution, but this action failed to silence her critics, one of whom commented, "We've been living under a dictatorship for twenty years. What's a little while longer?"

On the question of the U.S. bases in the Philippines, she also seemed to waver. As a leader of the opposition, she had signed a statement calling for the removal of foreign military bases on Philippine territory. During her presidential campaign, she had said that the United States could keep the bases until 1991 when the lease would expire, adding, "Since many events may occur between now and 1991, we shall keep all our options open." As president, however, she softened her position, saying that she supported the "eventual removal of the bases," but refused to set a date. The issue of the bases, she said, should be put before the Filipino people to decide by a vote. She herself was willing to negotiate a longer lease.

Vice President Salvador Laurel began issuing statements about Cory's inability to govern. "We don't have the luxury of time," he said. "The people are getting impatient and hungry." When asked to rate President Aquino after one hundred days in office, Laurel gave her "an A for effort and sincerity." But he added, "No results yet can be perceived at this point."

President Marcos's running mate, Arturo Tolentino rated President Aquino "somewhere about sixty percent . . . not quite passing." Tolentino tried unsuccessfully to overthrow President Aquino in July 1986, but his one-day coup failed.

The new leader even took flak from Ferdinand Marcos, the man she had deposed. After calling President Aquino "the worst dictator the world has known," Marcos offered to return from Hawaii to help fight the communist insurgents. President Aquino rejected his offer. "I think I can handle the insurgency problem," she said.

For months, Marcos's supporters rallied every Sunday, calling for Aquino to be ousted. President Aquino said she knew that Marcos phoned them from Honolulu to egg them on. Asked if she was worried about that, she replied, "As long as he only uses the telephone, why should I be worried?" Laughing, she urged the U.S. government to make sure that Marcos paid his phone bills.

Despite her good humor, President Aquino showed signs that the pressure was getting her down. She said that she would not run for president again if the new constitution called for elections. She maintained that she would remain in office just long enough to stabilize the country and to prevent Marcos from returning.

She appeared flustered, stuttering several times when asked what she had accomplished during her first one hundred days in office: "Well . . . and we have also started . . . well, I think another very notable achievement is that finally we Filipinos are proud to be Filipinos."

The U.S. government continued to express support, but there was concern in Washington about her ability to hold on. Senator Joseph Biden, a Democrat from Delaware, said, "No matter how good she is, she is almost incapable of meeting the expectations of the Filipino people."

For some Filipinos, expectations did not include much change. "The Philippines is a corrupt little country," one Filipino observed. "Everyone gets paid off under the table. If you want to get a package from the post office, you have to wait in line and pay off the guy. How can she change that? It's always been that way, even before Marcos." He added, "Of course, compared to Marcos, President Aquino is very honest. That's why she's popular. But not everyone in her group is like her."

Head of State

The biggest problem facing President Aquino was the $26 billion debt left over from the Marcos era. Worsening poverty and an unemployment rate of nearly 40 percent contributed to the overall crisis. President Aquino was afraid that the communists would make even bigger gains if the economy didn't show some sign of improvement, fast.

Knowing that her government was very popular with the Reagan administration, President Aquino headed for Washington on September 15, 1986, hoping to convert her popularity into financial support.

The Reagan administration had initially suggested that she visit the United States in November, but President Aquino was not alone in sensing that the situation at home was already critical. Emmanuel Pelaeza, the Phillipine ambassador to the United States, agreed. "She had better come now that she's popular," he advised. "Later it may be too late."

The main risk in her leaving the Philippines was the threat of a military takeover in her absence. Defense Minister Juan Enrile kept railing against President Aquino for her efforts to negotiate with the communist rebels, calling her "soft on communism" again and again. Advisers and friends told her not to leave, saying that she would not be able to return to rule the country if she took this trip. But if she remained at home, she believed she was in a no-win position. If she went to the United States, she stood a chance of winning at least some of the money needed to get the country moving again. It was a gamble she knew she had to take.

This page and facing: Honoring Ninoy Aquino on the third anniversary of his death. August 21, 1986.

President Corazon Aquino and General Fidel Ramos review troops on Air Force Day. May 2, 1986.

Enrile assured her that he had no intention of overthrowing the government in her absence and placed the military on full alert to guard against trouble from Marcos supporters. Pro-Marcos groups were stepping up the frequency of their rallies calling for a "Miracle in September"—the return of Ferdinand Marcos from Hawaii on or before September 23 when Aquino was scheduled to return from her U.S. trip.

President Aquino addressed her people on television before she left the country: "Those who are afraid that my absence will endanger the democracy are those on whom we cannot depend to protect it, for democracy here is not held up by me alone, but by the power of the people who won it."

As her plane taxied down the runway, a twenty-one-gun salute sounded across Manila airport, where just three years earlier President Aquino's husband, Benigno, had been gunned down.

Corazon Aquino's trip to America stood in sharp

contrast to the visits by Ferdinand and Imelda Marcos in 1966 and 1982. President Aquino and her aides traveled business class on a commercial Philippine Airlines flight to San Francisco. In 1982, the Marcoses had chartered two 747 jumbo jets plus a mammoth military C-130 aircraft to carry equipment and people to appear at pro-Marcos rallies in America. The Marcoses sealed off the first-class section of one of the 747s to use as their bedroom and dressing room. Imelda brought two hundred pieces of luggage, and their entourage numbered seven hundred people. That trip cost millions of dollars. On just one shopping spree in New York City during that visit, Imelda spent $200,000.

President Aquino and her fifteen-member delegation brought only two suitcases apiece to avoid paying any baggage surcharge. The trip was expected to cost less than $500,000. The press corps of about one hundred Filipino journalists accompanying President Aquino did not get a free ride from the government, as they had when Marcos was president. This time their news organizations paid their expenses.

"Co-ry! Co-ry!" About six hundred people, many of them wearing yellow, Corazon Aquino's trademark color, welcomed her to San Francisco with signs saying, "We Love You, Cory," and "Aquino: The Philippines' Woman of the Year." A U.S. Navy band played rousing music.

"I thank the American people for their prayers and cheers as we advance toward freedom," President Aquino told them, recalling that when her husband Ninoy arrived in San Francisco after having spent more than seven years in jail, "the color came back into his cheeks. That's the effect of freedom on anybody who's been denied it too long." Then she stepped forward to shake hands with members of the crowd while wary Secret Service men stood guard.

Then it was on to Andrews Air Force Base in Maryland aboard *Air Force Two,* one of the presidential airplanes. Arriving in Washington by helicopter, President Aquino stepped down to the floodlit lawn in front of the Washington Monument to be greeted by more chants of "Co-ry! Co-ry!" Secretary of State George Shultz took a yellow handkerchief from his pocket and waved it at President Aquino, who smiled back at him.

U.S. officials were looking forward to President Aquino's visit. One said, "She's done one hell of a job, considering the problems she has. She is handling the problems, in our view, in an extremely competent and able manner."

President Reagan heaped praise on her, too. "President Aquino has been doing her level best to unite her richly diverse people under a banner of freedom and opportunity," he said after the two leaders met privately at the White House. "Her efforts to reconcile all elements of her society and bring them into the democratic process are applauded here." President Reagan then assured her "that all America wants the Philippine democracy to succeed and to prosper. And we'll do what we can to help."

President Ronald Reagan greets President Corazon Aquino at the White House. September 17, 1986.

As he spoke, dozens of Marcos supporters shouted, "Down with Aquino!" and "Cory is a communist!" but President Reagan continued, "I'm bullish on the Philippines," a reference to a "bull" or positive stock market. "I will hope American and foreign investors take note of this incredible opportunity to help build a country." After all, he said, President Aquino's efforts had "inspired the world and won the hearts and imagination of people everywhere."

In response, President Aquino said she was "gratified that President Reagan understands and supports what we are trying to do. From this meeting today, both our governments will go out with a clear sense of priorities . . . that we must both work hard to strengthen the bonds between us." She added, "I hope we have set the tone and direction for a new relationship."

White House aides thought they had. If the goal of President Aquino's visit was to forge a strong personal rapport between the two heads of state, then the White House meeting "had certainly achieved that," said one official.

Corazon Aquino stopped the show on Capitol Hill the following day when she addressed a joint session of Congress. Although members of Congress usually wear drab blues and grays, on that day, September 18, the chamber was alive with flashes of yellow as the senators and representatives sported yellow ties, vests, and blouses. Congressman Jim Wright, the House majority leader, had

President Corazon Aquino at White House luncheon. To the left of President Reagan sits Vice President George Bush. To the right of President Reagan sit Secretary of State George Shultz and Defense Secretary Caspar Weinberger. September 17, 1986.

President Corazon Aquino addresses United Nations
General Assembly. September 22. 1986.

ordered two hundred yellow rosebuds for the legis-
lators to wear in their lapels. And the familiar
chant, "Co-ry! Co-ry!" rang forth from the gallery.

Looking bright and confident in a yellow suit,
President Aquino received a standing ovation that
lasted more than a minute. She was interrupted by
applause eleven times, and many members were
close to tears as she delivered a speech that some
hailed as "the best ever delivered in Congress."

"Three years ago, I left America in grief to bury my husband," President Aquino began. "Today I have returned as president of a free people." She described the tumultuous election and thanked Congress for "balancing America's strategic interest against human concerns." Declaring that "ours must have been the cheapest revolution ever," President Aquino promised that "as I came to power peacefully, so shall I keep it." And she said that although she did not want to resort to "the sword of war . . . I will not stand by and allow an insurgent leadership to spurn our offer of peace and threaten our new freedom."

She received another standing ovation as members of Congress rushed forward to shake her hand.

"The entire presentation had a magic to it that was really extraordinary," said Senator Richard Lugar, chairman of the Foreign Relations Committee. "It was one of the highest moments I've ever seen in the chamber."

Republicans and Democrats agreed. "She captured the hearts of a lot of people in that room" said Republican Senator Paul Laxalt. "She touched all the right heartstrings," echoed Democratic Congressman Larry Smith.

As he was escorting her out, Senate Majority Leader Robert Dole told President Aquino, "You hit a home run."

"I hope the bases were loaded," she replied.

They certainly were. Later that day, the House voted 203 to 197 to grant $200 million in emergency aid to the Philippines. (The aid package was later approved by the Senate.) One congressman,

Republican Toby Roth, objected, saying, "Yes, President Aquino gave a very excellent speech today, but is it worth a quarter-billion-dollar honorarium?"

President Aquino also fared well with the financiers of the World Bank and the International Monetary Fund, securing a $300 million loan from the World Bank and $500 million from the International Monetary Fund. She then arranged for further talks to reschedule payments on her country's mountainous foreign debt.

"There are no more Marcos cronies with their hands in the till," President Aquino explained. "There are opportunities that are ready to be started with fresh capital and fresh management." She pointed out that a climate of political freedom was healthier for economic growth.

All across the United States, President Aquino made one triumphant stop after another. In New York City, she told alumnae and students at her alma mater, the College of Mount Saint Vincent, "I would never have believed that I could face the thousands and the millions of people and give them my message. Most of my classmates remember me as a shy girl." At the United Nations headquarters, she told the General Assembly, "The rights we fought for are universally sought . . . enshrined, not entombed, in the U.N. conventions."

In New Jersey, a check for $300,000 and the papers to a $1 million estate were turned over to President Aquino by U.S. lawyers who had found property belonging to the Marcoses. A United

President Corazon Aquino meets with United Nations Secretary General Javier Perez de Cuellar. September 22, 1986.

States court had ruled "that assets of the government of the Philippines had been converted by the Marcos family and its associates to their own personal use."

In Boston, she received an honorary law degree at Boston University and revisited her old home. Homeward bound, President Aquino again stopped in San Francisco, where she visited with elementary schoolchildren who released yellow balloons into the air and greeted her with the familiar chant, "Co-ry! Co-ry!"

She listened attentively as a boy named Mihn Luu read an essay on "What Freedom Means to Me." Luu was one of the Vietnamese boat people who escaped with his life. "I know what freedom is because I come from a place where there is no freedom," he had written.

President Aquino responded, "I think it is good to know, at an early age, what freedom is all about." Asked what freedom meant to her, she said, "It means a lot to me. That's why I'm here to ask the American people to help us preserve the freedom we restored in our country."

Another student asked how she liked being a mother, grandmother, and President. "I like being grandma best of all," smiled President Aquino.

But she had less time to be simply a grandmother when she returned to the troubled country she called home. Rumors of an impending military takeover continued to simmer. Every week new reports from Manila predicted that President Aquino was about to be overthrown by the military because of her failure to "get tough" on the communists.

But she held firm, insisting she would exhaust all peaceful means before resorting to "the dramatic surgery of war." She noted that Ferdinand Marcos had used the military to fight the communists for twenty years and had still failed to contain them.

In addition to inheriting the problems of the Marcos era, President Aquino had her hands full with some new ones of her own. At the top of the list: overseeing the drafting of a new Constitution, to be followed by new elections to reinstate the National Assembly. There was also the possibility of another Presidential election. Although she had said earlier she would not run again, she told aides that the admiring crowds in the United States had made her feel she was really a leader. "More than ever, I really feel I am president now," she said. Aides noticed another change in her. Whereas she used to leave her office door open and encourage wide-ranging informal discussions on many subjects, after her overseas trips, "she became more remote, more distant, more presidential."

But whether she would have time to mature fully as a president was one of the biggest questions hanging over her. Even with increased aid from the United States, the road ahead looked rocky. But, Corazon Aquino had beaten the odds before. Analysts tried to predict how long she would last but they could only say that her presidency could end tomorrow or could last for several years.

In November 1986, rumors that she was about to be overthrown increased in intensity. Defense Minister Enrile was reported to be plotting to unseat her at any moment. Rumors rippled through the press. Once again, President Aquino's every move was broadcast all around the world by satellite.

And once again, President Aquino decided not to listen to her advisors who told her not to travel abroad. Again in search of more financial help President Aquino determined to visit Japan. She hoped to be able to convince government officials and businessmen there to invest in the Philippines.

Cardinal Sin arranged a meeting between President Aquino and her Defense Minister before her departure. "Their quarrel was similar to that between a husband and wife," said Sin, who counseled both of them not to argue in public because it would confuse people who looked to them for leadership. Defense Minister Enrile assured Presi-

President Corazon Aquino is welcomed by Japan's Emperor Hirohito in Tokyo. November 10, 1986.

dent Aquino that he would guarantee the stability of the country in her absence. He phoned her every day during her trip to inform her about the military situation at home.

On November 13, the day she returned home, with promises of increased aid and investment, Rolando Olalia, a prominent leftwing labor leader, was found murdered. Olalia, who headed the country's largest trade union as well as a newly formed leftwing political party, had three days earlier promised to support President Aquino if the military attempted to seize power. Olalia's colleagues suspected that it was the military who killed him.

President Aquino's government immediately dispatched twenty-one teams of investigators and offered a reward of $10,000 for information leading to the arrest of Olalia's killer or killers.

Several days later, five men armed with pistols kidnapped Nobuyuki Wagakoji, a Japanese businessman who worked in the Philippines. Nobuyuki, the first Japanese to be kidnapped in the Philippines, was abducted as he was coming off a golf course. Since no political motive was immediately apparent, his kidnapping appeared aimed at destabilizing relations between Japan and the Philippines and at undermining President Aquino's success in obtaining financial commitments from the Japanese.

More than 100,000 people turned out for Olalia's funeral. Thousands joined in a general strike intended to shut down Manila. The strike was not as effective as its organizers had hoped it would be, but made a point nonetheless. A spokesman for

Olalia's labor federation said that the protests were not directed against President Aquino but were meant to urge her to be more decisive.

"If Mrs. Aquino had acted swiftly to curb military extremists, Olalia's murder would never have happened. This will affect Cory badly because the people will lose faith in her," said one Olalia supporter. A spokesman for Cardinal Sin observed, "It almost doesn't matter any more whether or not a coup is staged. The damage has been done: The whole world believes that the Aquino government is teetering dangerously on the edge of the precipice and the slightest nudge will send it crashing down."

In the days that followed, a former political ally of Defense Minister Enrile was assassinated, two police chiefs were gunned down and seven bombs exploded in Manila's crowded shopping districts. The Manila police chief said he thought it was part of a campaign to create chaos. "Maybe they think because I am a woman they can scare me," said President Aquino. "I'm determined to make a success of this government."

On November 23, after an emergency cabinet meeting, President Aquino announced that she was firing Defense Minister Enrile and asking the rest of her Cabinet to resign. This was not "Mrs. Nice Guy." Her hair was pulled back from her face and dark shadows ringed her eyes. With new severity, the president announced, "Of late, my circumspection has been viewed as weakness, and my sincere attempts at reconciliation as indecision. This cannot continue. It is clear that the extreme left has no interest in the peace I have continually offered. I have, therefore, given the government negotiating panel until the end of the month to produce a cease-fire or terminate all further negotiation."

She continued, "This morning I summoned the Cabinet to a special meeting. I directed all Cabinet members to give me their resignations. Those who do not do so I shall nonetheless consider resigned. Almost all have tendered their resignations. I am expecting the remaining few to do so by the end of the day. This will give the government a chance to start all over again. I have accepted the resignation of Minister Enrile and have appointed Deputy Minister Rafael Ileto to be the new Defense Minister. We need a fresh start."

As the plot behind the president's action unfolded, General Fidel Ramos, the low key Chief of Staff of the Armed Forces, emerged as the man who had saved President Aquino's government. It was Ramos who had reportedly uncovered a plot by about 180 people to overthrow President Aquino.

A spokesman for the president said that "a dagger" had been plucked from the Aquino presidency. Plotters had intended to take over the National Assembly building and reinstate the Assembly which President Aquino had disbanded. The plotters were primarily Marcos supporters and disgruntled military men, the spokesman explained. However, their plan to reinstate the legislature and call for presidential elections was only a ruse. "That was just a ploy." he said. "Eventually their target was to bump her off." This was not the first time

President Aquino had learned of a plot against her life. On the eve of her departure to Japan, she had been told people were plotting to kill her.

President Aquino's move to take control of her government was hailed around the world. The United States government was relieved but not surprised at how she overcame this most difficult crisis of her presidency. "We were fairly confident of the essential realization by most people that she represented the best hope for the country and we relied on the common sense of the military leadership," said one U.S. official, adding, "things are in much better shape now." The State Department said that it had no information that former Philippine President Marcos had been involved in the reported coup attempt. They indicated, however, that the United States government would not allow him to remain in Hawaii and attempt to overthrow another government.

In Manila, some military officials questioned whether or not the threat of a coup was real. Some said that General Ramos had used the rumors of a weekend coup to force President Aquino's hand. Even the new Defense Minister, General Ileto, conceded he had no hard evidence a coup was going to take place. "I'm not doubting," Ileto told reporters. "I'm not saying the word doubt. I just want to be reassured that there is such a thing."

The Asian countries neighboring the Philippines were not concerned about whether the attempted coup was real. They viewed President Aquino's move to take control as positive. Even the pro-Communist Chinese newspaper in Hong Kong said,

"In recent months, Enrile's ambition for supreme power has been thoroughly exposed. His removal has temporarily allowed the Philippines to avoid a coup and to restore calm." Hong Kong's capitalist *South China Post* said about Enrile, "Mrs. Aquino gave him plenty of rope. He has hanged himself." But it also warned against "the bristling spears of a military increasingly aware of its power." Newspapers in Bangkok criticized President Aquino saying, "If Aquino is to be faulted it is that she allowed him (Enrile) a free rein for too long."

Some political analysts in the United States felt that the long-term crisis was far from over. "Enrile may not have got what he wanted in the way that he wanted it, but he got what he wanted," said one analyst. "He got fired, which means he can now lead the opposition. He'll bounce back."

President Aquino didn't seem to think so. With new confidence, she told a crowd, "It has often been said that Marcos was the first male chauvinist to underestimate me. He was not the last to pay for that mistake." And, referring to Marcos's earlier remark about a woman's place being in the bedroom, she said, "It is not I who have been consigned to the bedroom of history."

TEN

Six More Years

The new year began with smiles and accolades. President Aquino, a woman, was honored by *Time* magazine as its "Man of the Year" for 1986. On January 19, she won the Martin Luther King award for nonviolence. The award was named for slain civil rights leader Martin Luther King, Junior.

In a statement issued from Manila, President Aquino said, "Despite all the wars that have been fought in the name of democracy, democracy's essential values are peaceful and are best attained and preserved by peaceful means. Inspired by the courage and the victory of Dr. King, Ninoy found the courage to stare death in the face and to shed his blood as an investment in liberty."

President Aquino's own investment in her nation's liberty remained on shaky ground. The previous weekend, the military in Manila had been placed on "red alert," full military preparedness. Again, rumors of an attempt to unseat her swirled around the capital.

A main street leading to Malacanang Palace was barricaded by about twenty soldiers. An anonymous phone caller threatened to throw a hand grenande at the church-run radio station that had supported Aquino's "people power" campaign. Several Manila newspapers reported that the security alert was aimed at Moslem rebels and Marcos loyalists. "We cannot afford not to react and take precautions, Defense Minister Ileto said. "Rumor or no rumor we have to take the necessary measures."

During the security alert. President Aquino was on the road, drumming up support for the new constitution. The forty-eight member commission appointed by President Aquino had completed work on a draft of the new charter in October 1986. If approved by a national vote, scheduled for February 2, 1987, the new constitution would replace the so-called "Freedom Constitution" which President Aquino had declared one month after taking office. The "Freedom Constitution" had disbanded the National Assembly which was packed with Marcos supporters and superseded the Constitution of 1973 in which Marcos had developed what he called "constitutional authoritarianism." President Aquino had come under fire for doing away with this Marcos-era document.

If voted into effect by the Filipino people, the new constitution would reduce the power of the President, reinstate the two-chamber National Assembly, and strengthen the judiciary branch of government. It would also give President Aquino an automatic six-year term of office without separate

Presidential elections. A vote for the constitution would be, in effect, a vote for her.

President Aquino was hoping the nation would remain calm through the elections. But on January 22, trouble struck again. A group of protesters demanding land reform staged a protest near Malacanang Palace. The demonstrators, members of a leftwing farmers' rights movement, were calling on President Aquino to begin land reform by redistributing land owned by her own family. The protesters were angry, and some carried clubs and knives.

When the demonstrators surged towards the soldiers that formed a barricade, some of the soldiers began shooting. In the mayhem that followed, protesters began running away, screaming while shots continued to ring out. Bodies lay strewn on the ground, many shot in the head and in the back. Reporters covering the protest rushed in to help, carrying the wounded to hospitals while the shooting continued around them.

Initial reports said that twelve people had been killed. But several days later, the final death toll rose to eighteen with ninety-four people wounded. Also wounded was public confidence in President Aquino, the woman who had promised, "As I come to power peacefully, so shall I keep it."

One of the leaders of the farmers' protest said bitterly, "The fall of the Aquino government has started." A Manila journalist predicted that the killings marked the beginning of "the downhill slide" for President Aquino. Members of the leftwing groups called her "repressive." Those on the right called her "weak and incompetent."

In a separate development, political opponents of President Aquino released tapes of her telephone conversations with members of the constitution-writing commission. Although she had promised that the commission would be independent, the tapes reportedly showed President Aquino breaking that pledge to pressure commission members about nuclear bases in the Philippines, a project favored by U.S. military interests. An Aquino spokesman said that the embarrassing tapes were made by members of the military, who were supposed to be making sure the telephone lines were secure, not tapping them.

President Aquino announced an investigation into the January 22 shootings and warned of more trouble ahead, claiming that anti-Aquino elements were trying to destabilize her government eleven days before the critical constitutional referendum. "Attempts to destabilize the government and defeat our democratic aim will intensify," she warned. "We are prepared for this contingency."

From his exile in Honolulu, Marcos predicted that "Madame Aquino cannot last several months." He insisted that his hands were clean. "I am not doing anything and look at the insane happenings in my country. You can't expect me to sit here idly while the Philippines comes under the iron heel of an alien ideology." He said he wanted to go home but Aquino's Cabinet had voted unanimously against him doing that. Nonetheless, he promised that one day he would return and "try Aquino and all the others for their dastardly acts committed against the Philippine republic."

Looking ahead to the February 2 elections, Marcos forecast a 2 to 1 vote against ratification. He accused President Aquino of removing electoral inspectors from different political parties and said, "She may not get the mandate she is looking for unless she cheats. If there is massive cheating, there will be the beginning of a massive civil war."

Four days later, the panel investigating the shootings gave a preliminary report: troops loyal to Marcos were the guilty ones. The order to fire on civilians had not come from President Aquino or soldiers loyal to her.

That same day, January 26, 1987, more than fifteen thousand people gathered for a new march on Malacanang Palace. This time, they were marching to protest the previous week's shootings. But this time, President Aquino ordered the barricades lifted around the Palace and kept soldiers away from the demonstrators. This time, she dispatched around eight cabinet ministers to link arms with the protesters and lead them to the palace gates. "We can say now that Malacanang is truly for the people," said one of the rally's organizers.

"It's part of the process of healing," Trade Minister José Concepcion commented.

"You see, all the senior officials of this government are here to make a point, that this government is committed to peace," added the manager of the government television station.

"If she had done it earlier," grumbled a peasant leader, "Blood would not have flowed."

Said President Aquino, "I'm glad it's over."

But it wasn't. More trouble was brewing.

That same evening, computers in newsrooms around the world started to beep as bulletins began coming over the major news wires. "Troops Seize Two Television Stations in Manila," reported Reuters at 6:41 P.M. Eastern Standard Time. "Troops in full battle gear seized two Manila television stations and troop movements were reported in various parts of the city," read the first dispatch from the Philippines.

Were these soldiers defecting from the Aquino camp, maddened to the point of mutiny by the killings of the week before? Were they perhaps loyal to some new military junta in the making? First reports were sketchy, then a few clues surfaced. At 6:47 P.M. Eastern Standard Time, Associated Press reported that "soldiers surrounding the television station came from a military region north of the capital. The troops were wearing red and blue armbands." The north was Marcos country and red and blue were Marcos colors. It was the most serious attempt to grab power from Mrs. Aquino since she came to power.

Twenty-four hours later, government troops were locked in a standoff with the rebel faction still holed up in the complex housing Channel 7 television and a radio station. About 160 rebel soldiers, a few police officers and about 50 civilians loyal to Marcos had taken over the station as part of a larger attempted coup that included staging attacks on five military garrisons around Manila. Defense Minister Ileto reported that one rebel was killed and 16 wounded in the attempt to seize power. Police and soldiers had arrested 271 conspirators and at least 70 more remained at large.

Earlier that day, about 300 Marcos supporters rallied near the TV station complex. Lighting fires and throwing stones at police they shouted, "We want Marcos! We want Marcos!" Government troops fired tear gas and smoke bombs at the crowd which dispersed briefly then returned to taunt police and soldiers. At least 34 people were injured and 6 arrested in the fighting.

President Aquino addressed the nation on television that evening. Urging calm, she announced, "The situation is well in hand," adding that the rebels would be well advised to surrender. "Their situation is hopeless. Every moment of delay merely compounds the gravity of their crime." Taking a stern tone, she warned, "Let me make myself clear on this matter. I have ordered the chief of staff to proceed against the officers responsible for this act of rebellion in accordance with the manual of courts martial. The full force of the law will be applied to everyone, civilian and military, who is implicated in this crime. I have ordered their arrest and detention. There is a time for reconciliation and a time for justice and retribution. That time has come."

"Don't let this get worse, declare your surrender," shouted one of Aquino's officers outside the station the following day. "The Filipino people are asking you to please think this over thoroughly so we can solve this problem. We beseech you to come out."

Then he delivered an ultimatum: "Surrender in thirty minutes or else!" The one thousand government troops surrounding the station readied their weapons. A convoy of five military trucks filled with soldiers in gas masks and heavy combat gear rumbled towards the station. Marines wearing yellow armbands stood by, ready to storm in. After the thirty minutes were up, troops fired four tear gas canisters at the station. The rebels did not come out. Instead, they continued broadcasting their demands over the radio station: retirement of overage military officials; fair treatment of all troops, including Marcos loyalists; reorganization of the armed forces; permission for others to demonstrate in support of the rebels; and no use of force against them. Unless those demands were all met, they said they would not surrender.

But the following day, after six hours of negotiations, they surrendered peacefully, exiting the station waving cheerfully to their supporters outside. First they gave up their ammunition, then boarded military buses for the trip to army headquarters where they yielded their weapons.

President Aquino reiterated that the civilians would be charged with rebellion and military personnel would be court-martialed. "It was a clear attempt to overthrow the first principle of democracy—civilian supremacy," President Aquino said during a speech interrupted many times by applause. "We will have justice."

Around the same time that the siege at the TV station complex was ending, reports about Ferdinand Marcos's role in the incident began to surface. When asked on Tuesday night whether he had directed the attempted coup, Marcos had answered, "No, no, no, no." But in fact, a charter jet belonging to an Arab oil sheik had been standing by in Honolulu during the TV station siege in order to take Ferdinand and Imelda back to the Philippines.

Philippine government officials had requested the U.S. government to intervene. A State Department envoy visited Marcos' home in Honolulu to inform the deposed dictator that he would not be allowed to leave. The U.S. government had evidence that Marcos was behind the attempted coup, the envoy said, reminding Marcos that he would be held to his agreement not to go to the Philippines unless invited by the Philippine government. "I feel now I am being treated like a prisoner," Marcos responded. "I will do everything possible and legitimate, even at the risk of my life, to try and reach the Philippines, to try and help our people."

Marcos's previous homecoming preparations included the making of a videotaped message to send to his supporters back home. It showed Ferdinand Marcos working out in a pair of boxer shorts and doing leg raises in a green sweatsuit. Marcos made the tape to convince critics that he was really in good health, explaining to the audience, "All these propaganda ploys, these fabrications that I am supposed to be dying, that I'm in a convalescent state and I will not be able to come home are false and fabricated." Intended as a New Year's greeting, the tape was intercepted before it reached the Philippines.

To prepare for her return trip home, Imelda had gone on one of her legendary shopping sprees. This time, she spent more than $2,000 at a store specializing in paramilitary clothing. Imelda bought camouflage military pants, Israeli-made combat boots, olive drab T-shirts, flight jackets and some Navy jackets with fur linings. Asked about Imelda's purchases, Ferdinand Marcos explained that they were made for their household security staff in Honolulu.

Cory Aquino had survived another onslaught. But as the elections approached, many questioned her ability to hold on. "Philippines President Cory Aquino seems to have survived a second coup attempt, but the sequence cannot fail to hurt her— and at a moment when her authority was already taking a heavy battering and when she needed every ounce of political strength at her command," said a *Washington Post* editorial. "Once again the fragility of Philippine democracy was painfully underlined."

Fragile perhaps, but Philippine democracy triumphed again on February 2, when 80 percent of all registered voters turned up at the polls. A strong campaign by both Aquino and opposition camps had been urging everyone to vote. Signs reading "God said, 'Vote'" sprouted in cities and villages.

It was an unusually calm election day by Philippine standards. There were some reports of thugs intimidating voters in two provinces but no election-related fighting and, this time, nobody was killed. Speaking from Honolulu, Marcos accused the government of offering low-level government workers about five dollars each to vote *for* the constitution. The Aquino government charged Marcos supporters with offering people about two dollars each to vote *against* it.

President Aquino was among the first voters, casting her ballot near her family's sugar plantation. She promised that the constitution would bring stability and economic recovery. Asked whether the Philippine people would approve the constitution, President Aquino said, "Yes, we will."

And they did. The first returns showed a two to one margin in favor of the new constitution. The final vote was 76 percent in favor with 22 million people voting.

President Aquino was now more than a transitional leader. The Philippine people wanted her to serve six more years. Six years in which to help the country recover economically while balancing the many different opposition factions. Six years in which to change the government infrastructure dominated by Marcos appointees. Six years in which to guide the Philippine people towards peace.

It would be a stormy six years, no doubt. With Marcos still eyeing the country he left behind and his supporters ready to take up weapons behind rabble rousers. President Aquino would need to keep watch at all times. Negotiations with the communists broke down on January 22. Shortly before the cease-fire was due to expire, on February 8, the insurgents started killing again—five soldiers were killed and five wounded in one day. The insurgents said they were taking action against what they called the "imperialist" constitution.

The communists had "bared their fangs to our peace-loving people" with their "hardline position and impossible demands," declared General Ramos as he ordered his troops out in pursuit and planned pre-emptive strikes against the insurgents. "If we do not act on this, it will pose a great danger to civilians." However, he repeated that the door to further peace talks was open and said that all military action would "follow the decisions of the civilian leadership."

Discouraged by the failure to maintain the cease-fire with the communists, President Aquino none-theless pressed ahead with her reconciliation campaign. Her representatives held peace talks with Moslem separatists whose fourteen-year war had claimed more than sixty thousand lives. The Aquino government was willing to consider the Moslems' request for a separate, autonomous state in the south.

Overall, President Aquino remained optimistic. "The tremendous vote of confidence reaffirms the now unquestionable legitimacy and democratic power of our government," she announced after the first results were in. "Our people have spoken and they have commanded us to rule by law, and anyone who challenges that law must answer to us."

Asked why she believed she was elected in the first place, President Aquino answered, "Because I was the widow of Ninoy, and also because I am Cory Aquino." No longer was she the shy little wisp hanging around the kitchen. Corazon Aquino had long ago realized that although humility was a virtue, self-confidence was a necessity, especially for a woman president. "I have to project my confidence even more than most men would," she observed.

She had taken power in a wounded nation, with the mandate not just to govern but to heal. It was a tall order for anyone. But if the problems she faced were monumental, so, too, was her "spiritual staying power"—President Aquino's personal definition of courage. Her indomitable spirit made her a formidable leader, who cared for her people.

Could Cory do it? The world was watching closely for the answer. Whatever the outcome, Corazon Aquino clearly understood her obligation: "My philosophy is to do everything within your capability and leave the rest to God. I have honestly been living that way since Ninoy's incarceration. No one can say Cory did not give it her all."

Index

About The Author

Laurie Nadel has been a writer since 1969. Her work has appeared in *Natural History, Columbia Journalism Review, Signature, New York Times, The Times* of London, and other major publications.

She has also worked as television news writer in London and New York City, where she presently writes for CBS News.

As a reporter for *Newsweek* and United Press International, she covered the 1973 military coup in Chile and American oil exploration in the Amazon jungle. She was the first woman reporter to visit an oil company base camp in the heart of the jungle.

En route to becoming a writer, Laurie Nadel has worked as a dental assistant, waitress, secretary, translator, researcher, comic book censor, taxi driver, photojournalist, and reporter. She has also worked as a television news producer.